A SAINT
ON DEATH ROW

ALSO BY THOMAS CAHILL

THE HINGES OF HISTORY™

How the Irish Saved Civilization

The Gifts of the Jews

Desire of the Everlasting Hills

Sailing the Wine-Dark Sea

Mysteries of the Middle Ages

A Literary Guide to Ireland (with Susan Cahill)

Jesus' Little Instruction Book

Pope John XXIII

2

A SAINT
ON DEATH ROW

The Story of Dominique Green

THOMAS CAHILL

NAN A. TALESE

Doubleday

New York   London   Toronto   Sydney   Auckland

Published in the United States by Nan A. Talese, an imprint of
The Doubleday Publishing Group, a division
of Random House, Inc., New York.
www.nanatalese.com

DOUBLEDAY is a registered trademark of Random House, Inc.

Grateful acknowledgment is made to the following for permission
to reprint previously published material:
"This Be the Verse" from *Collected Poems* by Philip Larkin. Copyright © 1988,
2003 by the Estate of Philip Larkin. Reprinted by permission of Farrar, Straus
and Giroux, LLC, and Faber and Faber Ltd., London.

"More Than Just a Rosary" reprinted by permission of *National Catholic Reporter*,
115 E. Armour Blvd., Kansas City, MO 64111. *NCR* Web site: NCRonline.org.

Library of Congress Cataloging-in-Publication Data
Cahill, Thomas.
A saint on death row : the story of Dominique Green /
Thomas Cahill. — 1st ed. p. cm.
1. Green, Dominique, 1974–2004. 2. Death row inmates—Texas—Biography.
I. Title.
HV8701.G74C34 2009
364.66092—dc22 [B]
2008036329

ISBN 978-0-385-52019-5

PRINTED IN THE UNITED STATES OF AMERICA

1   3   5   7   9   10   8   6   4   2

First Edition

In memory of

Raymond E. Brown

Ursula M. Niebuhr

Jacqueline Kennedy Onassis

kind, courageous friends

If you are not loved, you do not exist.

— MARIO MARAZZITI

A SAINT
ON DEATH ROW

PROLOGUE

I first met Dominique Green in December 2003. Right after our meeting, I wrote this account of my impressions.

He moves with an athlete's grace; and his gestures, though economical, are expressive and dramatic. In repose his face has the dignity of a Benin bronze, and yet it is quickly animated by spontaneous displays of sympathy, humor, concern. Lights flash playfully in his dark eyes; he smiles and laughs easily. His quiet brow shows no effort or anxiety, but his eyes, when concentrating, seem to look beyond the present to a better world that only he can see. His countenance is suffused with an aura that, if one did not know something of the harshness of his history, might be mistaken for innocence. It's not innocence but goodness. His conversation is the most amazing thing about him: lively, liquid, without uncertainty, without cant or jargon, alive to the presence of his visitor but patiently pressing our dialogue in the direction of his own profound concerns. It is unusual—at least outside ancient literature—to come upon his combination of intelligence and simplicity, suggestive of an untrammeled soul. He seems a born leader with no hint of the trivial about him and so devoid of the mundane concerns that weigh down most of us that you would feel no surprise to hear someone predict that, mark my words, this fellow will one day take his place as chief justice of the United States or archbishop of Canterbury or secretary general of the United Nations.

But Dominique Green can be none of these things. He is, rather, an inmate who lives in the solitary confinement of a six-by-nine-foot cell for twenty-three out of every twenty-four hours along the infamous Texas prison corridor called Death Row. When he is permitted a visitor, the visit must take place in one of a row of tiny visitors' booths, each booth divided by a window of double glass through which prisoner and visitor may observe each other but never touch. In order to converse, the two must make use of telephone receivers attached to the walls.

Dominique is where he is for two reasons only: because he is poor and because he is black. Raised in an alcoholic household by a mother whose idea of discipline was to burn the palms of her children's hands, living on the streets of Houston from the time he was fifteen, Dominique was no angel—nor should the society that failed him utterly expect him to have been. At eighteen he was involved, it would seem, in an armed robbery with three other boys. The victim pulled a knife.

There was a struggle and one shot was fired, killing the victim. The only independent eyewitness did not identify Dominique as the killer. The police did a deal with one of the boys—the only white one—that left Dominique charged with, and soon convicted of, capital murder. The white boy, never charged with anything, went free, and the district attorney interfered with investigators attempting to interview him; the three blacks went to prison. Dominique alone was sentenced to death after testimony from a psychologist known to believe that African Americans and Latinos are more prone to violence than others are likely to be. This psychologist was chosen by Dominique's court-appointed attorneys, who appeared—even to the victim's wife—to work hand in glove with the prosecutors. These attorneys failed to introduce evidence that there had been a struggle (which would have led to a conviction for manslaughter, rather than murder), nor did they request DNA tests of any kind.

Over the eleven years Dominique has lived on Death Row, where he will soon reach the end of his appeals, he has grown from a neglected and abused boy into a man of stature. At first, he was full of self-hatred and hatred toward all those who had helped land him where he was. But the year-in, year-out faithfulness of a young woman who refused to let Dominique sink into a cauldron of despair finally brought him to his senses. He began to look around him and to take inspiration from older inmates; he began to read, to write poetry, and to draw. His reading has brought him to every category of fiction and nonfiction. He dislikes only fantasy, an understandable prejudice for someone in his situation. He has become a man not only of learning but of wisdom.

Not long ago, he read Archbishop Desmond Tutu's book *No Future Without Forgiveness*, about the archbishop's experience as chairman of South Africa's unique experiment, the Truth and Reconciliation Commission, during whose sessions perpetrators of political violence were encouraged to tell the truth about what they had done in the course of the apartheid era, and the victims of that violence (and their families) were encouraged to forgive those who repented their violence. Dominique was deeply impressed by the book and realized that this was the path he and his fellow inmates must take. He pressed the archbishop's book on anyone who would have it. (You may wonder how it is possible for men in solitary confinement to converse with one another and to share things. Since it would be a transgression for me, who was told many things in confidence, to describe the prisoners' methods, all I can say is that human beings are infinitely inventive.)

Under Dominique's leadership many, perhaps even most, of the inmates on Death Row in the State of Texas have now forgiven everyone who has harmed them and, insofar as they can, have asked forgiveness from those they have harmed. Dominique is convinced that he has a vocation to inspire the kids who turn up on Death Row to drop their petty hatreds and to morph into larger, more generous human beings—in the same way that older inmates, since executed, once provided spiritual models for him to follow. Of course he would love to be free, but he also knows he has found his role—a meaning and purpose for his life that no one can take from him.

When I visited Dominique this first time, it was mid-December. The prison was full of Christmas decorations and the sounds of staff and visitors wishing one another merry Christmas, happy New Year. I asked Dominique what Christmas was like along Death Row. For the only moment in our long conversation, his eyes filled with tears. We share with one another, he said, and those with no money to buy anything from the prison commissary are given gifts of food by more affluent inmates. ("Affluent" is an exceedingly relative term in this context: there are no millionaires along Death Row, nor will there ever be.) We even have a sort of feast with each one sitting by the door of his cell, surrounded by his gifts, as present to one another as we can be. In all, it is a wonderful day, said Dominique; and all of us, both givers and receivers, feel better about ourselves.

Gifts. Good wishes for the future. Sharing what we have. Taking comfort and strength from the presence of others. Feeling better about ourselves. Surely, this sums up what everyone wants from Christmas. As I left Dominique and made my way along the metal corridors, waiting for each of several locked doors to spring open and bring me a step closer to freedom, I caught a glimpse through a pane of bulletproof glass of a tiny crèche displayed on a table: stable, donkey and cow, sheep and shepherds, and the central group of father, mother, and child—marginalized figures of poverty and ethnic disparagement in their time, forced to take a long, uncomfortable journey in the woman's ninth month of pregnancy in order to satisfy the state and its need to wrest from poor people the little they had. Then, having reached their goal of Bethlehem, there was no room for them anywhere and they were forced to spend the night of the child's birth in a cattle stall. Their world was harsh, a world where men were crucified for no good reason (supposing there can be a good reason to crucify anyone), a practice that would one day claim the precious little baby the woman had just given birth to.

Were they bitter, this man and this woman, bitter about the world they found themselves in, bitter about the lot they'd been assigned? Did they wonder if God had abandoned them to be permanently oppressed by the rich, the powerful, the careless, the unfeeling? No, I reflected, their lives were not confined to the politics or circumstances of the moment, however appalling. They had faith that, as the woman put it, God would one day "rout the proud of heart, pull the princes from their thrones and exalt the humble, fill the hungry with good things and send the rich away empty." They were so sure this would happen that they lived as if it had already come to pass. And, besides, they had a brand-new baby, who made them so happy they could almost hear angels singing, "Peace on earth, good will to all."

That angels' song, faintly discerned more than two thousand years ago in Bethlehem, may still be heard this Christmas, not perhaps in your local shopping mall or around your Christmas table or from the choir loft of your local church.

These are the places where we try, usually unconvincingly, to reenact the first Christmas, the real Christmas. But without doubt it will be successfully reenacted at Polunsky Unit, Livingston, Texas, by forgiving people no one wants, who live bravely in the Valley of the Shadow of Death, comforted and encouraged onward by a man with a face both simple and luminous.

1

The man known to me as Dominique was born Dominic Jerome Green in Houston, Texas, on May 13, 1974, the first child of Emmitt and Stephanie Faye Smith Green. This was less than four months after my own first child was born. As in all our lives, the most important truths of our histories come to us through the uncertain lenses of remembrance, viewpoint, and self-justification. It is always hard, and often impossible, to sort out what actually happened from the way it is remembered either by the subject himself or by those closest to him. But having listened to several witnesses to Dominique's early life, I set down here the truest account I can frame of his early years.

That Stephanie was a mother from hell seems to be taken for granted by everyone. But the truth of this portrait is open to question at least in some of its particulars. How did Dominique, who looked so much like her, who possessed her intelligence and even her cunning, evolve into the expansive human being he became if all his early experiences were negative? Mothers mold us more surely than do all others. In his earliest years, Dominique's mother was a different woman from the creature she became. Our most damning evidence against her comes from the 1980s, and there are no incidents related of her before 1981 that would force us to name her an abuser of children.

I met Stephanie and spent several hours with her in mid-July of 2007. There can be no doubt that most people would find her evasive, narcissistic, and creepy. The row of gold-capped teeth that glint from the front of her mouth, combined with the quicksilver indirection of her responses, can almost leave the impression that you are speaking with an android, a counterfeit human being.

Stephanie was brought up in a household that she claims was in league with the devil, a family devoted to the worship of Satan. Certainly, her mother was a practitioner of voodoo and believed she could put curses on other human beings and magically control them. Stephanie was forced as a child to have sexual relations with several, perhaps all, the mature males of the household and of her extended family. When she was barely into her teens, she gave birth to a baby girl, the result of one of these encounters. Her mother took the baby and raised it as her own and threw Stephanie out of the house before she was fifteen.

Despite this terrible beginning, Stephanie was able to function as wife and mother at least for a while. From the first, she acted the part of the dominant parent, Emmitt always assuming the more passive role. Defining herself in contrast to her mother's grotesque religious practices, she attended her local Catholic church and had her children baptized there. Stephanie surely admired her first baby: "I remember this little guy about nine months old tottering across the floor on his feet. He's nine months old and he's walking, O.K.? I remember this little guy who used to have a beautiful smile. He was smart as a whip. He could do anything he set his mind to. He'd do it. He was always leading stuff."

In 1976, two years after Dominique's birth, his younger brother Marlon, another handsome child, was born. The two boys became inseparable companions and, soon enough, co-conspirators. Stephanie and Emmitt would have a third child, Hollingsworth, but not till 1985. By then, the cracks in their lives had become too obvious for anyone to miss.

When Dominique was six, two supposed friends of Emmitt broke into the house, intending to rape Stephanie and kill Dominique and Marlon in retribution for a drug deal gone wrong. They did not succeed. But when Dominique was seven, another episode of violence left its invisible scars: Dominique was raped by a priest at St. Mary's, the Catholic school he attended in Houston. Though his mother withdrew him from the school, she failed to inform either the police or school or church authorities. She did not even tell Emmitt, nor did she arrange for a medical checkup for her son. From this time forward, the life of the Green family started to disintegrate as Stephanie, succumbing to the nightmares of her own history, began to ignore her children and enter into the world of destructive madness she has inhabited inconstantly ever since.

It is a common experience of sexually abused children that they come to think of themselves as disposable beings of no account. That, after all, is what those closest to them have shown them they are worth, that is what society has reinforced by its silent nonintervention. All that is required is for such children to internalize this external judgment of others as the value they place on their own lives. They become zeros—and they begin to act out their own emptiness. This is why sexual abuse of children is often labeled "soul-murder."

Of course, this process can be short-circuited and even reversed if there are people in a child's life, especially parents, teachers, and similar figures of authority who stand up for him, telling the child—by word and especially by deed—that he is valuable, that the rape (or lesser abuse) was an evil exception that should not be factored into his own judgment of himself.

It may be that Stephanie was whole enough, courageous enough, to ward off for a time the judgment that her family of origin had placed on her, but that an attempted rape and the attempted murder of her children, followed by the rape of her firstborn son by a sacral figure in whom she had placed her trust, was too much for her to withstand. The rape of Dominique, especially, may have so troubled her that she could not recover her equilibrium.

She descended into alcoholism, began to prostitute herself for money—in full view of her children—and alternately ignored and persecuted them. She was especially hard on the eldest, who stood up to her and resisted her bizarre impositions and demands. She beat him, scorned him as weak, demeaned him as "the black sheep." She had come to hate him, as she hated herself, for having been raped. Emmitt, never a bulwark but nonetheless a skilled musician who taught Dominique to play drums and guitar, turned into a full-fledged drug addict, absent in mind if not in body—a characteristic casualty of the 1980s. About this time, Emmitt's mother, Dominique's loving grandmother, died. She was the adult Dominique had been closest to and felt protected by. One would think that the familial landscape could hardly become more bleak.

And yet, life continued to worsen. "Alcoholism," Dominique would recall much later, "changed my mother. It ate up her mind and slowly destroyed her heart. No longer was she that loving and caring mother I once knew: she became very hateful, bitter, and unfortunately abusive. All the memories she'd repressed, all the things she went through in life, came back to haunt her in full force." The household was now awash in booze and drugs, and unsavory visitors often lurked nearby or within the precincts. Phone calls were often received from pushers, pimps, and johns. When Dominique, who had just recently learned his letters, received one of these calls and failed to write out a message for his mother, she punished him by holding the palm of his right hand over a gas flame. It was a close replay of something her own mother had done to her. A few years later, Stephanie would punish Dominique in the same way again. Luckily, Dominique was left-handed (which his mother bullied and taunted him for), but he carried the ugly scarring from these incidents into adulthood. When Dominique was nine, his father gave him a gun for self-protection.

By the time he reached eighth grade, Dominique resolved to be known by the name he would bear from then on: he was no longer "Dominic," the name his mother had given him at his birth; he was reborn as "Dominique," the name he had given himself. It was a token of the growing resolve of this boy to take control of his life, to act as his own man.

A year later, in 1989, Stephanie and Emmitt separated; in the same year, Stephanie suffered a head injury at the Nabisco factory where she worked and had to be hospitalized, after which her behavior deteriorated further. In one incident, she shot at Dominique with a pistol because she thought he had left a metal knife in her microwave, which then exploded. It was actually the five-year-old Hollingsworth who had done so, but Dominique, observing his mother's hopped-up condition, took the blame for the explosion. Before she went for the pistol, little Hollingsworth, foreseeing what would happen next, managed surreptitiously to empty the pistol of its bullets. Stephanie would attempt to shoot Dominique on one more occasion but succeed only in shooting up her own car, which was parked behind him—her sons finding this an occasion for hilarity.

In 1990, Stephanie was admitted to a mental institution, the first of several such admissions, and she was diagnosed as schizophrenic. When her children visited her, she claimed not to recognize them. The children were left at home alone to cope as best they could. Dominique was then beginning to get into trouble with the law and found himself sentenced briefly to a juvenile detention facility because he had been found with a small quantity of marijuana and an illegal weapon. That summer, Stephanie, in one of her visits home, tried to have Dominique placed in juvenile detention again, along with Marlon, her middle child. Failing to achieve this objective, she kicked both boys out. In the same summer, Emmitt, at a new job after a spell of unemployment, roused himself at last and obtained custody of all three sons. But Dominique, "so hurt," as he put it, refused to board with his father and, resolving to find a new way to manage, dropped out of sight.

For a time, Dominique crashed with friends, then spent some weeks in the open with a homeless man, who taught him the ins and outs of sleeping under the highway or in abandoned cars. Finally, Dominique rented a storage shed as a place to live. He was finished trying to abide Stephanie. Though he had left home on a number of occasions in the past, this time he had no intention of returning. He was also finished with school. After the rape at St. Mary's, he had attended a public elementary school, then two different middle schools, followed by three different high schools. Though he was smart and intellectually curious, the goal of education, as it appears to normal children, could have no appeal for him.

He hoped to avoid additional stints in juvenile detention, where he had been sexually abused by staff, especially on visitors' days when no one ever showed up to see him. While other children were receiving visits from family members, Dominique was lying on his bed in a pool of his own blood, which leaked from his torn anus. Pedophiles, always drawn to jobs that entail unsupervised work with children, are also keenly aware of which children lack adult protection. (A series of reports in the *Dallas Morning News*, beginning in February 2007 and picked up by newspapers such as the *New York Times*, has brought to light that the sexual abuse of minors has long been pervasive in Texas's institutions for juvenile correction.)

In his late twenties, Dominique would look back on his personal experience of sexual abuse in a poem entitled "What does hate create?":

> I watch him
>> cry out
>> stretched out
>> turned inside out
> and nobody does anything
> no one utters a peep
> but everyone knows what happened
> and feels the tears that pour down his face
> understands the pain that dyed his sheets with blood
> from hungry erections injecting him with hate.

Next to this poem, he would one day draw a surrealistic picture of the boy these rapes had made of him, a tense, tearful child out of whose eyes grow thorny stems that end in fantastic flowers—a multivalent image that incarnates the tension between the child's private aspirations and the pain of his reality.

Just sixteen, Dominique knew his fate was now entirely in his own hands. But he also meant to do whatever he could to protect his brothers, an obligation he took with high seriousness.

Both Marlon and Hollingsworth remain full of memories of Dominique's protective role in their early lives. Hollingsworth, eleven years younger than Dominique, remembers him as "a loving, honest, true friend, a mentor, a leader," who took him to clothing stores and toy stores and to the amusement park to ride the go-carts and the little trains. He played basketball and football with Hollingsworth and his friends and was always "very gentle." Marlon recalls being afraid of the dark and Dominique descending from the upper bunk bed to lie next to him till he'd fallen asleep. "He was almost like my second dad. He did a lot of things that a father should do and my mom couldn't do." Dominique tried to teach Marlon how to withstand Stephanie, how not to give in to her in his mind. "About the time that Mom started getting physical, he was like a human shield almost," Marlon remembers. "He deflected a lot of stuff that was directed towards us from my mom [and from] a couple of my teachers. He served as a buffer. She told us that she really didn't want us, that she wished she had never had us. After that, it was just him and me against the world." Emmitt himself admitted in an interview in 2003 that Dominique cared more for his brothers than did he and Stephanie.

How would Dominique at sixteen continue to protect these brothers, at the mercy of mad Stephanie and inconstant Emmitt? Part of the solution would lie in earning sufficient money. He had already had some experience selling drugs; now it became his livelihood. "I chose the drug trade," Dominique would write later, "because I didn't have the nerve to be a burglar, the heart to be a jacker, the cunning to be a thief, the will to be a pimp, or the hate to be a hired killer. I was just a kid trying to find a way for me and my siblings."

Given the household he came from, he was hardly unfamiliar with drugs. He had sold them from the age of eight, once dealers recognized that cute little Dominique could serve as the perfect pusher. When he was nine, his mother began taking half his drug money from him, as if he were working for her. More than once, he had even sold drugs to each of his parents. He had gotten high on pot at thirteen—to find out what the experience was like—but the idea of taking drugs regularly held no allure for him. It was a business, the only one he knew.

He had begun somewhat inauspiciously by selling white candle wax, which he refashioned to resemble rocks of crack cocaine, but soon he was embedded in the brisk trade that fed the crack epidemic. "Dominique," says Marlon, looking back, "wasn't selling drugs so he could go out and buy flashy cars or anything like that. He just wanted the money so we could live."

But if there is no honor among thieves, among drug dealers there is only shame and violation. Even Dominique, motivated by love of his brothers, could not escape the coarsening effects of such employment. And with the epic disappointments of his family life and the natural aggression that the advent of puberty can work on even the mildest of boys, the face that Dominique began to show the world was one of brutality and rage, a rage that would not abate for many years. For all that, his rage was eloquent, coherent, and full of grown-up resolve: "I promised myself that I would never sell myself short for anyone ever again. I stopped caring about people because those that I did care about did not care about me."

Some, such as his brothers, however, continued to receive the considerate gentleness that had previously distinguished Dominique in all his dealings. Another recipient of Dominique's positive attention was Jessica Tanksley, a captivatingly beautiful neighborhood girl, two years his junior, whom he would soon begin to court with extraordinary deference and ceremony. She would be duly impressed. But Dominique also impressed his juvenile probation officer, Sylvia Gonzales, who remembers him as "always well behaved" and extremely likable. "There are certain kids that you never forget," Sylvia would remark many years later. "They just get to you—to your heart."

At sixteen, Dominique's rather realistic assessment of his own strategy was that eventually his drug distribution business would land him in prison. He hoped only to remain free as long as his brothers needed him. Then, he reasoned, after he finished serving his time, they would be old enough to take care of him when he returned to rebuild his life. As his bad luck would have it, however, he was to remain free only till he was eighteen.

2

On October 18, 1992, Dominique Green was arrested by the Houston police. It was his fourth arrest. He had been driving a stolen red car the previous afternoon when the police gave chase along a fifty-mile stretch of Highway 288. The car ended in a ditch in Brazoria County, just outside the city. Dominique, lightning quick, set off on foot through field and forest and succeeded in eluding capture till the next day, when the police sent out dogs to track him down. Arrested immediately were two others, Michael Neal and Mark Porter, both black, who were found in the backseat of the car in possession of a large handgun and a BB gun. The handgun was sent off for ballistics testing.

The police, aware of a recent series of armed robberies carried out at a shopping mall and elsewhere by young black men, believed they had caught the perpetrators. In lineups, one or another of the arrested men was then identified by witnesses; and though no one identified Dominique, the three prisoners were charged with participating in robberies. Michael Neal, however, represented by counsel arranged by his mother, was able to put up a bond for his release.

The ballistics test came back, establishing that the handgun, a Tech 9, was the weapon that killed a man named Andrew Lastrapes Jr. outside a Houston convenience store in the early morning of October 14. Eventually the police, questioning the suspects separately, determined that Mark Porter could not have been part of the group that morning, but that two other youths were: Paul Lyman, black, and Patrick Haddix, white. Neal did not provide a statement at that time.

At this point, for anyone researching the history of these events, the record becomes exceedingly muddled and incomplete. How the police made the determinations they did and why the various suspects were charged and brought to trial could defeat the deductive skills of the most prescient investigator. This is only partly because seventeen years have passed since these events. It is also because the State of Texas keeps shockingly incomplete records of such matters and because many of those in authority are unwilling or unable to shed any light on the matters in which they were participants. Sandy Melamed, for instance, who was appointed Dominique's lawyer, told Sheila Murphy, a retired Chicago judge who would eventually become involved in Dominique's appeals, that he drank a couple of Scotches every night and that, well, his recall just wasn't very good. He was far more forthcoming than most.

Much of what I can report comes not from those in authority but from the accused perpetrators and from the family of the victim. Andrew Lastrapes, according to his wife, Bernatte, was a "truly good man," a big black truck driver who always kept a few dollars in his pocket for beggars. But he was also a man who kept a knife on his person and knew how to use it—and he would never have surrendered his wallet without a fight. After his body was turned over to his family, Bernatte discovered that his back pants pocket where he kept his wallet had been torn and that there were puncture wounds in one of his hands, both suggestive of a struggle. The obvious scenario is that Andrew resisted the robbery with his knife and was shot in a scuffle. He lay in the parking lot for hours, alive and bleeding. It is hard to resist the speculation that he might be alive today if the police had seen fit to call an ambulance in a timely manner. But it is also hard to ignore the possibility that the shooting of Lastrapes was an unintended consequence of the scuffle. Such mitigating possibilities were never shared with the jury.

Though Melamed was appointed to defend the indigent Dominique on robbery charges, Dominique was soon charged—on January 5, 1993*—with capital murder by a Harris County

---

* The abysmally sloppy press release from the Office of Attorney General lists the date as January 5, 1992—*before* the murder occurred. The legal record contains not a few such errors.

grand jury, despite the fact that his prints were not found on the murder weapon. (Someone else's were, someone never identified.) But the police, after many hours of intense grilling, finally wrested a signed "confession" from Dominique by making empty threats to arrest Stephanie. Dominique, not wanting his mother arrested and his family even more wrecked than it already was, told a story of his involvement that he believed would be subsequently discredited by witnesses and fingerprints. "Bart," he claimed, had been the killer. Bart did not exist—or, to put it more precisely, no one with that legal name was found.

Texas treasures a legal wrinkle within its "law of parties" according to which any participant in a crime that results in murder may be charged with the murder, even if he or she had nothing to do with committing the murder. The statute reads in part: "All traditional distinctions between accomplices and principals are abolished by this section, and each party to an offense may be charged and convicted without alleging that he acted as a principal or accomplice." Under this statute one might expect that four young men—all seen by the police as participants in the robbery that resulted in the death of Andrew Lastrapes—would be put on trial for capital murder. But this was not the case. Only Dominique, the youngest and least protected, was so tried.

Michael Neal was protected by his lawyer; and both Neal and Paul Lyman were able to plea-bargain their way to more limited sentences. Patrick Haddix, the sole white participant, was never booked or charged with anything, merely characterized as a "citizen informant." To read in succession the sworn statements that Dominique, Lyman, Porter, and Haddix gave to police is to be struck as if by a blow. The statements of the three black boys are typed in the usual police manner: all in capital letters, all full of typos and grammatical and spelling errors. Haddix's statement is typed with extraordinary refinement in upper- and lower-case letters, and its language is startlingly literary, even elegant. The writer of this prose punctuates and paragraphs perfectly, knows how to write dialogue, even employs the semicolon correctly. The statement, which reads like fiction, is full of novelistic detail and runs to five dense pages, whereas the others' statements have the clunky, halting sound of teenage accounts and range between one and three poorly typed pages. To compare Haddix's supremely polished statement with the unfocused, inarticulate, fear-ridden, stop-and-go courtroom performance he gave subsequently is to know that this statement, recorded many hours after the statements of the others, was not written or dictated by Haddix but provided by an expert, hired to engineer an intended outcome.

At the time the ballistics report came in, both Neal and Lyman had been released and only Dominique, unable to post bail, remained in custody. The most likely scenario is that Haddix, first to point the finger at the others (while never denying that he had acted as lookout and had shared in the proceeds of the robbery) and having much better family connections, was able to wiggle free of the legal vise that ensnared the others. But only Dominique, the least experienced, the least able to mount a defense, was left exposed to the death penalty that the police and the legal system were determined to impose on *someone*.

Complicating this picture is the nature of the only testimony against Dominique, which was supplied by the other three. According to them, Dominique and Neal got out of the car and walked toward Lastrapes, who was getting out of his truck in front of the convenience store, while Lyman and Haddix pulled the car around to the back. So only Neal, not the other two, could know what happened when Lastrapes was confronted and which of the two—Dominique or Neal— shot Lastrapes. But also: since when are co-conspirators who are doing a deal for a lesser sentence (and, in the case of Haddix, no sentence at all) found credible in a court of law? In the entire history of law and in every country that takes law seriously, the testimony of co-conspirators who exculpate themselves while implicating another is viewed with suspicion.

The United States Supreme Court has termed such testimony "inherently unreliable." Even Texas has an "accomplice witness rule" that requires corroboration of such testimony before it is admitted. But, as an exceedingly experienced Texas attorney confided to me, "the corroboration tends to be anything that matches the prosecutor's theory of the case. Almost anything serves, eviscerating the purpose of the rule."

Dominique's trial was over almost before it began. Melamed, originally appointed by Judge George Goodwin of the 174th District Court to defend Dominique against robbery charges, now petitioned the judge in the new capital murder case—

Doug Shaver of the 262nd District Court—asking that he be allowed to continue to represent the defendant. Melamed had only one previous brush with a capital murder case: he had been second-chair defense attorney in a famous Harris County case known as "the sleeping lawyer case," which had been argued before the same Judge Shaver who was to preside over Dominique's case.

In the earlier case, the principal defense attorney, one John Benn, then in his seventies, had been seen by those present to sleep throughout the trial, his eyes shut, his mouth repeatedly falling open, his head lolling back on his shoulders. When asked about his behavior, Benn defended himself impatiently. "It's boring," he whined. What makes the case famous, however, is not that the lawyer slept (which was hardly a first for Texas) but that Judge Shaver remarked dismissively to the *Los Angeles Times*, "The Constitution says everyone's entitled to the lawyer of their choice, and Mr. Benn was their choice. The Constitution doesn't say the lawyer has to be awake."

Shaver, who had been Melamed's mentor, readily agreed to the lawyer's request that he continue to represent Dominique. There was a second lawyer on Dominique's "team," Diana Olvera, who has never since allowed herself to be interviewed about this case. But keep her in mind; she will appear in our story once more.

The jury, composed of whites and one Asian American but of no blacks or Latinos, had no trouble convicting Dominique. Bernatte Luckett Lastrapes, who attended the trial with her father, a pillar of Houston's black community, and her eldest son, was shocked at the cursory nature of the proceedings and the lack of substantive engagement and effective participation by the defendant's lawyers. Bernatte began to wonder if this was really a trial at all or rather some kind of bizarrely predictable ritual with a predetermined outcome. She noted that Dominique's mother, who attended, slept through almost the entire proceeding. Poor Dominique, thought the murdered man's widow. He has no one.

At the least, Dominique's attorneys must be judged exceedingly bumbling and naïve. Knowing little about Stephanie, Olvera appears to have supposed that a mother would help sway the jury to sympathy. She asked Stephanie if she thought her son capable of such a crime. Yes, proclaimed Stephanie with considerable assurance, he's just like me. For her day of testimony at her eldest son's murder trial, Stephanie managed to call forth one of her more evil personae. But her testimony weighed heavily on the jury in deciding to convict Dominique of murder. After all, even his mother was against him. Later, when asked what Dominique's punishment should be, she urged the court to inflict on her son whatever punishment the law allowed. Though this second outburst was instrumental in ensuring that Dominique would be given the death penalty, the jury was told nothing of Stephanie's schizophrenia or of her repeated hospitalizations in mental institutions.

Melamed and Olvera did call another character witness, Sylvia Gonzales, Dominique's juvenile probation officer, who was sympathetic to Dominique and recognized the extremely negative role Stephanie had played in his young life. Sylvia testified briefly to Stephanie's oppressive behavior toward her son as well as to Dominique's character, "easygoing and receptive," "truthful and cooperative." But Sylvia was not prepared to testify by Dominique's lawyers, who met her but once—in the hallway just prior to her testimony—and they made little of her testimony.

Far more important was another character witness, a supposedly scientific one. For the sentencing phase of the trial, Melamed called a psychologist, Dr. Walter Quijano, to testify to Dominique's psychological disposition. Quijano, who was born in the Philippines and whose father was of Spanish (not Hispanic) ancestry, has in other cases urged the death penalty for explicitly racial reasons, believing, as he does, that the race of a defendant—if the defendant is black or Latino—is a "statistical predictor of future violence." In Dominique's case, Quijano, keeping quiet about his racial prejudices, limited himself to telling the jury that Dominique had never developed a normal conscience and could therefore be a future danger to society if he were allowed to live—this from a witness supposedly testifying on behalf of the defendant. Though Quijano had interviewed Dominique briefly, his assessment came not from anything he had learned directly in his interview. Rather, his assessment of Dominique's lack of conscience was a syllogistic deduction: those who grow up in circumstances like Dominique's—that is, without a caring parent—lack a normal conscience; therefore, Dominique lacks a normal conscience.

But in the end, race was hardly absent from these proceedings, as the most damning evidence in support of Dominique's punishment came from his own words. Before he had been charged with murder, he had written a letter from jail to Mark Porter (who had been found by police in the stolen car that Dominique had been driving) in which he suggested a narrative they could propose of their movements, a narrative that would enable them to elude conviction ("how to get our case dropped or at least dropped down"). The letter is partly written in ghetto-speak, perhaps because eighteen-year-old Dominique thought he was being cool but also perhaps for the sake of rendering it difficult for any authority intercepting the letter to make sense of it. It begins playfully: "What's up damn fool?" The rest of the letter is the "story" (whether accurate, invented, or somewhere in between, I cannot verify) of what Dominique and his friends were doing the night of the murder, mostly looking for girls and getting into arguments with other boys. The letter ends casually with an expression of Dominique's unconcern as to whether Porter and the others will go along with this or not: "I don't care if a nigga with me or not 'I forever be a trigga happy nigga.' " To me, this looks like a pose of unconcern and bravado, masking anxiety.

The last words, a quotation from a then popular rap song, "Trigga Happy Nigga," by a Houston group, the Geto Boys, were placed in double quotation marks by Dominique—a plain signal from the detail-oriented author of the letter that he is quoting *someone else's words*. Read aloud in court by the prosecutor, however, these words signed Dominique's death warrant. The members of the jury, needless to say, were not informed that what they were hearing was a literary quotation, designated as such. By his own words, Dominique had convinced the jury of the murderous danger that society would be "forever" subjected to, if he were allowed to live.

Normally in a court of law, a letter is read aloud after its recipient has testified that he received the letter and identified from whom it came. But the presence of Mark Porter on the witness stand might have pushed the case into unpredictable byways. He almost surely knew things that the prosecutor did not wish the jury to hear, things that might have bearing on Dominique's possible innocence (such as that all the codefendants knew one another, one of many facts kept from the jury). The prosecutors found a simpler course for introducing Dominique's letter: they asked his mother to identify his handwriting, which she did. On July 9, 1993, a Harris County jury found Dominique guilty of capital murder. On July 14, following the punishment hearing, the court sentenced Dominique to death.

Though the forces of law in Harris County are devoted to executing Death Row inmates with as much dispatch as possible, their eagerness is slowed somewhat by the venerable practice of appellate review, enshrined in the Texas state constitution and to which they owe at least formal loyalty. Over the years to come, Dominique would spend as much time as he could learning the intricacies of the law and of the legal processes by which he had been convicted and sentenced. Needless to say, his interest was hardly academic or disinterested. He needed to learn "the game," as he called it, the rules of which he had barely comprehended before and during his trial. For a long time he figured that there must be a legal key that would fit his case, that could unlock his cell and send him back to freedom.

He was held during these years in Death Row cells in two different prisons, at Huntsville, then from mid-1999 at Livingston (where he was held—as were all Death Row prisoners—in solitary confinement); and occasionally and for relatively short stays he was brought to the Houston jail. He had plenty of time for legal study. He met occasionally with one lawyer or another who was willing, usually for a brief period of time, to take up his case pro bono, that is, without compensation. On September 11, 1996, the Texas Court of Criminal Appeals (CCA) affirmed Dominique's conviction and sentence on his direct appeal. On November 13, it denied Dominique's petition for a rehearing. On April 28, 1997, the United States Supreme Court denied his petition for a writ of certiorari, that is, an order to call up and review the decision of the lower court. That August 29, Dominique filed an application in the state trial court for a writ of habeas corpus, which is an order to produce the prisoner in court for the purpose of investigating the lawfulness of his imprisonment. Its purpose, as used in the appeals process, is to uncover ineffective assistance of trial attorneys, misconduct by prosecutors or police, and previously unavailable evidence of innocence. Nearly three years later—on May 31, 2000—the CCA at last denied Dominique's application.

That these years were hard on Dominique is almost too obvious to say. He began his long imprisonment as little more than a boy, a street kid whose understanding of the world and its ways was severely limited both by his youth and his peculiar experiences. Over and over, he would say to anyone who would listen that he was innocent of the charge they convicted him of. For this reason he had rejected the offer prior to his trial of a thirty-year sentence if he would confess to the murder. But he also stated firmly that he would not become "a snitch." The impression he left was that he knew the identity of the shooter but would not identify him. He would speak darkly of those who had turned against him to save their own skins, but even this accusation was broached without his naming identifiable actors. Again and again, he reminded his attorneys that witnesses to the robbery spree that preceded the Lastrapes murder had spoken of three boys, not four, and he pressed the attorneys to locate the relevant videotapes made by the stores the robbers had passed through or near, including the videotape from the convenience store in front of which the murder had occurred. These, he claimed repeatedly, would establish his innocence.

He did admit being part of a gang of robbers on October 17, when the victim related to the police that one of the robbers apologized for what they were doing and thanked the victim. "What kind of robber tells a victim I'm sorry and thank you? One who didn't want to see any harm come to them. Someone like old friendly-ass me."

Through the worst of these years, Dominique kept his

sense of humor, though he often lost his temper. As year followed year without the hint of a reprieve, he snapped occasionally, sometimes more than occasionally, at friend and foe alike and certainly at his lawyers. For several years, he signed himself "Stumpa," his street moniker and the name under which he had performed aggressive, foul-mouthed rap songs (for which he had, just prior to his arrest, been offered a recording contract). For a while he tried to be a Muslim and wrote his name as "Dominique Green-El." But these glints of black-power rage tended to alternate with his natural optimism, his playfulness, and his capacity for enjoying the world, even the bit of it he could experience from his prison cell.

Through these years, he had a true friend on the outside, Jessica Tanksley, the delicately beautiful girl he had fallen for two years before he lost his freedom—and who is listed in court documents (with her assent) as Dominique's "common-law wife." Their correspondence is dramatic and humane; and though only Dominique's letters survive in quantity, we can hear Jessica's voice, as Dominique quotes occasionally from her letters. "Aint nobody ever told me things like you have. Like 'you know where home is.' Or tell me they love me and really mean it like you do. I aint never had anyone love me like you do. . . . And everytime you write me I continue to feel more needed and wanted. So when I come home to you, I want to be ready for you. And now I got all the time to prepare."

There are letters so intimate that to quote from them here would be a violation of privacy, but a paragraph from one of the less steamy ones will give you an idea: "Have you ever had a dream where me and you are together and I am kissing you, or you are kissing me? We slowly touch each other and hold each other. As I gently caress your skin that's so delicate and slowly move myself up to your breasts and start to nibble and kiss them and you. Then I feel you rub your fragile hands up my back and onto my face. I feel your hands softly rubbing up against my face. So I go down to embrace your lips and taste your breath and lick your tongue. But I wake up to find my own hand rubbing against my face. A pillow as the face I soon was to embrace. A sheet as the hand rubbing down my back. And a radio is the voice of you I imagined to hear."

To Jessica Dominique speaks openly of his worst fears: "I have visioned and thought about my own death over and over. And I know that when or if they take me to deathwatch to put me to sleep. Once my eyes close they will never open again. And I will only have three minutes to watch my life pass before my eyes. Watching all those moments I labeled precious, remembering all the things that brought me happiness, and also watching all my mistakes. Three minutes to recap and review my life.

"And not one time have I ever cried. I cried inside because the pain of being here is starting to kill me. But I do know that if I do have to go to deathwatch I wont show the pain then either no matter how bad it hurts.

"Baby, the shit fucks with me everytime I think about it. But I know that no matter what I wont hurt myself by becoming a snitch like these folks want me to be. Because then everything I have done or did would be a complete lie. That's why I cant say nothing and wont ever say nothing."

But Jessica is growing up in ways almost unimaginable to Dominique. In the summer of 1994 she leaves Houston to attend Xavier University in New Orleans. Her visits to Dominique, which had never been frequent because of the maddening difficulties that the inaccessibility of prisons places in the way of poor Texans, become even fewer. Soon she is writing about her courses and her reading in ways that leave Dominique in the dust. He is jealous and even confesses dislike of her then favorite writer, the long dead W. E. B. Du Bois, because she likes him too much ("—and I don't take second place for no one!").

In August 1999, however, this extraordinary correspondence comes to an end. Jessica, her bachelor's degree in hand, is heading to Havana to study medicine at the Latin American School of Medicine, having been granted a full scholarship by the Cuban Ministry of Public Health. Dominique, knowing that communication between a Death Row prisoner and a Havana resident will be almost impossible (and would subject Jessica to unwonted attention from the U.S. State Department), releases her from all obligations to him: "I wish you knew how hard this is for me, but for some small reason I think you do. Just like I think you knew I would eventually end up writing this letter." Just before this, he had written a harsh letter. But, "no matter how much I tried to make it seem like me, that last letter to you was someone I'm not. I know, and you know. I am a pussycat at heart. I ain't no hard-core muthafucka—although I wish I was. Thankfully who I am truly is a secret. A secret that can only exist between me and you. If anyone else knew, my bad boy image could end up being destroyed. Who knows I could cause a scandal and make these niggas here want to impeach me, like I was the president of some gotdamn body." (Earlier that year, President Bill Clinton had been acquitted of the impeachment charges against him.)

The self-deprecating humor cannot entirely obscure the immense generosity of this act of farewell. With Jessica gone from his life and his imprisonment entering its seventh year, Dominique, refusing to sink into despair, turns more than ever to his fellow prisoners and to the legal thicket of his case.

3

The Community of Sant'Egidio, based in Rome, is one of the very few great religious phenomena of our time. Most of us are so weary of fraudulent religious phenomena—the fake saints molesting altar boys in the sacristy, the preaching scoundrels, the rip-off charities, the feel-good evangelists who promise us both God and money—that we may have come to view all religious movements, perhaps especially *Christian* religious movements, with suspicion. When I first encountered Sant'Egidio, I kept asking myself if they could possibly be what they seemed to be. Any second now, I supposed, the clay feet would show themselves, peeking out beneath the concealing gown of righteousness. But now, having known many members of the Community for many years, I can report that they are in the main the real thing—the thing they say they are. I would like to spend a few pages telling you more about them because, despite their great distance from Texas Death Row, they are closely woven into the story of Dominique's life.

They started life as a ragtag assortment of Roman high school students who, inspired by the student protests of 1968, decided to meet in the evenings with the intention of becoming better friends and of finding ways to influence their society for the better. Soon enough, they discovered in the four gospels of the New Testament a sternly simple way forward. Jesus's repetition of the ancient Hebrew command, first articulated in the Book of Leviticus—"Thou shalt love thy neighbor as thyself"—became their program. They would obey this command by offering friendship—friendship to one another and to anyone else who fell across their path, especially anyone in need. (The Italian word for "friendship," *amicizia*, is built on *amico*, the word for "friendly" and "friend," which in turn is built on *amare*, Italian for "to love." So in Italian, as in the Latin that is Italian's predecessor, Jesus's command to love one's neighbor is more obviously a command to friendship than it is in English.) This was their antic "plan," a little absurd even to themselves. Smart, entitled middle-class kids, they were not entirely unaware of the potential ironies of simplicity, of how hollow their approach would sound to the cynical ears of fashionable Rome.

But they persevered. As they began to grow into a larger organization, they formed additional meetings throughout Rome, then throughout Italy. Often, the church halls where they tried to meet were shut to them by priests who thought their youthful spontaneity and priestless informality smelled of Protestantism. Soon enough, however, there were Sant'E-gidio communities in most European countries, then in Africa, Asia, and Latin America, the United States and Canada being the only region where Sant'Egidio remains relatively unknown. Though the headquarters of Sant'Egidio, close by the great Basilica of Santa Maria in Trastevere, keeps no record of numbers, there must now—forty years after their first meetings—be close to sixty thousand members throughout the world, perhaps less than half of them in Italy. Anyone who wishes to become a member, no matter his or her religious affiliation or lack thereof, national/ethnic background, or sexual orientation, is welcome. Anyone who wishes to participate in one or another of the Community's activities without becoming a member is also welcome.

All the communities meet for a prayer service, usually several times a week, that has scripture reading and a reflection by one of the members as its center. The chanted psalms and hymns they sing, though characteristic of them, seem inspired especially by the chants of Russian Orthodoxy, as is their use of an icon of Jesus that serves as the focus of attention. But the service, wherever it is enacted, retains a simplicity and an intensity that cannot but impress even the casual visitor. For many years, the original Roman community met for prayer in the Church of Sant'Egidio, a former convent of enclosed nuns that was given to them and from which the movement took its name.

Now, having outgrown its own church, the Trastevere chapter meets for prayer each night in the large Basilica of

Santa Maria, which is close to an apartment my wife and I own and where we spend a part of each year. Santa Maria, extraordinarily beautiful, is a mostly twelfth- and thirteenth-century building whose foundations are as ancient as the fourth century, when Christians first emerged aboveground to take their places as equal citizens of Rome and began to build the distinctive edifices that would ever after characterize the great city.

To stop at a description of the Community's prayer would be to falsify these people, for it is the works of Sant'Egidio at least as much as the prayer that distinguishes them. Though the original community in the heart of Rome contains many middle-aged members (as the students of '68 have grown gray and sometimes bald), its ranks have been continually replenished by people in their teens and twenties. Other satellite communities, of which there are more than a hundred in and around Rome, are more specialized: communities of the elderly, of poor working people, of gypsies. In each community, friendship with those in need takes precedence and consumes many hours of donated labor. Each night in Trastevere, for instance, fifteen hundred homeless people are fed at sit-down dinners served with graciousness and even style. Likewise, hundreds of substantial bags of groceries are distributed each week. The Trastevere community runs three refuges for abandoned old people, two AIDS hospices, a home for abused and abandoned children, and after-school programs for immigrants and others in the poorer parts of the city. It even runs a delightful, inexpensive restaurant—gli Amici (or Friends)—

in Piazza di Sant'Egidio, staffed entirely by mentally handicapped adults.

Each October, the Community organizes a torchlit March of Remembrance for the Roman Jews and all other Jews who perished under the Nazis. This march winds dramatically from the portico of Santa Maria and ends at the steps of Rome's great Synagogue. Almost as dramatic is the enormous feast for the poor that the Community hosts each Christmas afternoon inside the Basilica of Santa Maria.

More than fifteen years ago, members of the Community, believing they had a gospel responsibility to act as peacemakers, undertook a series of quiet, amateur efforts on their own and succeeded in arranging a peace in Mozambique between the guerrillas and the government (after sixteen years of war and one million casualties). The peace has held ever since. Not only did the Community go on to help achieve a similar, if less certain, peace in Guatemala, it continues to attempt reconciliation in Algeria, the Balkans, Burundi, Liberia, Ivory Coast, and other hot spots, working intuitively and patiently, never abandoning hope, and true to the belief that "war is the greatest poverty of all."

Each year, for more than twenty years, the Community has hosted an international interfaith conference in the hopes of building peace in troubled parts of the world by encouraging informal bonds of interfaith friendship and cooperation. At these conferences I have seen Arabs lunching with Israelis, Serbs dining with Bosnians, Irish Protestants drinking with Irish Catholics. Italian food and Italian wine are most helpful in establishing the right atmosphere—but above all there is the magic of Italian hospitality. As in so many of the Community's initiatives, the overriding goal is to quell hatred and division and to strengthen the bonds of community and fellow feeling wherever these can be encouraged.

The Community of Sant'Egidio has recently begun to build clinics for HIV/AIDS patients throughout much of sub-Saharan Africa, for which medical doctors of the Community train local staff. These clinics have already had signal success, especially in halting the communication of the virus from pregnant woman to fetus and in reaching more children than any other program in Africa. To help pay for its efforts, the Community has somehow lured the prosperous Italian wine industry into backing its Wine for Life program by which many of the best bottles of Italian wine sport a Wine for Life decal. The decal represents a small tariff on each bottle, which in turn supports the building and staffing of the African clinics.

As I read over the above paragraph, the thought presses upon me that to write that "the Community has somehow lured the prosperous Italian wine industry" is more than a little disingenuous. I know exactly how the Community has managed to do this: they have a secret weapon named Mario Marazziti.

Mario was among the first Roman teenagers to join the Community. Not as securely bourgeois as many of the other early members, he was orphaned fairly early. His mother died when Mario was six; his father, a piano player and erratic provider who sired children by several different women, died when Mario had barely finished university. Such experiences set Mario well apart from his contemporaries. I doubt there are any children on this earth better cared for than middle-class Italian children, who generally live with their parents into their thirties, can count on substantial trust funds to cushion their way in the world, and may even have their mamma installed as cook-housekeeper for the duration of her natural life. To find oneself cast out upon the world with little but one's own wits as weapons is an experience few middle-class Italians would be familiar with. It might be expected to leave an Italian boy crabbed, resentful, even permanently disoriented. It made Mario strong, graceful, and resourceful.

Now in his midfifties, Mario has what for lesser mortals might be considered three full-time jobs: a director of RAI, the national television service, he has recently been named president of a government-sponsored foundation that tackles problems associated with diseases of the blood that especially afflict people born in the Mediterranean region. (Like Tay-Sachs and sickle-cell anemia, these blood diseases can be found almost exclusively within certain genetically related groups.) Mario has been married for many years to another member of the Community, Cristina, a quiet, effective doctor, who is largely responsible for turning the African AIDS program into such a success.

Together, after fulfilling every jot and tittle of the long and excruciatingly difficult adoption process demanded by the Italian state, Mario and Cristina succeeded in adopting Andrea, a boy who came to them at last as a ten-year-old from the Community's shelter for children. There were, of course, a few rough patches in the raising of Andrea, who had no confidence in himself at the outset and required much shoring up by his adoptive parents. I recall Mario's intervening when a teacher told Andrea at the age of thirteen that he should give up school and "go to work." "*Professoressa stronza!*" exclaimed Mario under his breath, invoking the most vivid Italian slang. In his carefully composed letter to *la professoressa*, however, Mario merely suggested that *she*, not her student, would be well advised to seek another line of work, so as not to destroy teenagers just starting to bloom. Not long ago, Andrea graduated cum laude with a degree in the science of education from the Roman university LUMSA. Today, Andrea is himself a father—of little Matteo—and Mario and Cristina are what can only be called supergrandparents.

But being a grandparent, super- or otherwise, should never be considered a job. Mario's third job, which he has held for many years, is as *portavoce* (press spokesman) for Sant'Egidio. Whereas his first two jobs yield modest salaries, this third one, like all Sant'Egidio jobs, pays nothing. It was in this third job that he came in contact with Dominique Green.

Dominique told me when we first met that he had been advised by another Death Row inmate that, given his lack of familial support, he needed to look for a new family. Italy, the older man said, try Italy. The Italians are really bothered by the American institution of the death penalty. Maybe you could find support among them. Dominique took this advice and wrote to several Italian periodicals, asking for friends. One newspaper—*l'Unità*, at that time the Communist Party daily—translated his letter into Italian and printed it (as did a humor magazine, *Linus*, now defunct).

Here is Dominique's letter. Unfortunately, the original has disappeared. I was able to obtain only the translation into Italian, as published by *l'Unità* in March 1995. Though I have translated *l'Unità*'s Italian back into English, I can give no guarantee that the English words I have chosen are exactly the same ones Dominique used. This is as close as we can come to hearing Dominique's voice in his first attempt to move into the world beyond his prison cell:

Hello, my name is Dominique Green. I am a prisoner on Death Row. I have been imprisoned for three years and I am twenty years old. I am an African-American teenager and I have been condemned to death for murder. The only problem is that I did not commit the crime I was accused of.

And this is the reason I write: I need someone to help me. I thought you might like to help me to find someone who has the time to write to me or to help me—whichever they wish to do. Because in recent years I have not known exactly how to ask for help or for friendship.

I ask you now not only because the loneliness of this place begins to get to me but also because I realize that I can end up dead for something I did not do. Also this: the date of my execution is not yet set because my case is at the beginning of the appeals process.

I ask your help in this way: can you find someone who wishes to help me or simply someone who wishes to become my friend and to write to me? But if you do not wish to help me in any way, I thank you for at least reading my letter and allowing me to make something more of myself by telling you my problems. Thank you.

Stefania Caterina, a young member of Sant'Egidio, read this plea, underlining the words "simply someone who wishes to become my friend and to write to me." Though she was hardly in a position to do more than this, she answered Dominique's letter—but in her native Italian, not knowing that Dominique knew no language but English. Here is Dominique's response, exactly as he typed it on an ancient typewriter the prison allowed him to use occasionally. As in the letters to Jessica quoted above, the punctuation can sometimes be peculiar, but the letter also shows the first faint notes of the simple eloquence that would become the hallmark of Dominique's writing:

June 13th, 1995

Dear Stefania:

Greetings from many miles away! Many thanks for your letter, which I received today. I must say that it was good to hear from you, to know you're interested in trying to help. But unfortunately, I was unable to read your letter because it was not written in English. I am sorry for failing to state this to you in the newspaper article, but I hope that you will understand and still want to help me if you can. So, as I sit down to write this letter to you today. I hope that it both reaches and finds you in the best of health, thoughts, and spirits.

Since I knew that you do not know much about me, if anything. I would like to start this letter off by introducing myself to you. As you already know my name is Dominique Green, and I am a death row prisoner. I am an African-American male; 5 foot 10 inches tall; 158 pounds; and I have black hair and brown eyes. My birthday has just recently passed so I am now 21 years old.

I've been on death row since August of 1993. I'm accused of committing the death of a man while in the course of committing a robbery. My case, which is solely based on circumstantial/indirect evidence, is on appeal at the Texas Court of Criminal Appeals in Austin, Texas. But unfortunately, I do not have an attorney or any legal representation for my case. So that means that I can and may be executed or murdered at any given time, once my case can be ruled on.

Luckily, I met a person who was kind enough to see me struggling and try to help me. And their help to me was putting me in a place where only you could find me. So if you would want to help me then, and become my friend. You would know where to look. Because I am in need of not only someone that is willing to help me, but also someone who is willing to become a piece of my life.

If you do consider writing to me. I hope that you will come to me as yourself, and be yourself with me. So that we may possibly become close friends. Simply because I am on death row, and caged like an animal does not mean that I am a bad person. And I am that as time passes and our friendship goes through either good or bad times, you will see that I am a good friend to have, if not the best. But I also hope that you will be the same for me in my life, if not the best.

During my time here on death row I read and study the law sometimes, so that I may be able to better understand it. I also write poetry, read, and draw or paint in some of my free time also. Since I am also allowed a form of recreation to keep myself in shape. I play basketball* as much as I can also. But other than that my hobbies are blank, and my time is dedicated to my case. So I write trying to get people to see and understand and the injustice that has happened to me.

Stefania, I do not know what all that you can do for me, or will allow yourself to do for me. But I do know that even the least bit of your help would be greatly appreciated. Because I am trying to raise the money to hire an attorney to fairly represent me and my case once a ruling has been made on my case. And I really reed someone there for me who is really willing to help me, and not lie to me like most people and attorneys that I have met. If you are in a position where you could help me to some extent, your help would be

---

* This was before Dominique's removal to solitary confinement in Livingston in 1999.

greatly appreciated. But if you do not wont to do so, I'll understand. But please feel free to open your heart and share your thoughts with me, and even be yourself. Because I need for someone to come into my life and be my shining bright light, or my much needed last hope.

I hope that you will choose to write to me soon. But until then, please take care of yourself because I will be thinking of you. But for now I just would like to mostly thank you for taking the time to sit down and share your thoughts with me in the form of a letter.

Yours Truly,
Dominique

Stefania found a translator, who helped her overcome the language barrier, and the correspondence grew quickly into *"questa bella e profonda amicizia"* (this beautiful and profound friendship), as Stefania called it. *"Lui era come mio figlio. Lui era come mio fratello."* (He was like my child. He was like my brother.) Two people with what might have seemed an ocean of difference between them managed to connect almost immediately.

Stefania began to tell other members of the Community about her discovery of this engaging correspondent trapped on Death Row in Texas. Other members of the Community wrote to Dominique, as well as to other Texas Death Row inmates, to offer friendship. Soon enough, Dominique, as well as some of his fellow prisoners, had a growing circle of friends.

Surely, thought these new friends, there must be something more we can do for these men. As time went by, members of the Community began to visit the prison—not an easy thing to do because the State of Texas restricts severely visits to its Death Row. But a young priest of Sant'Egidio, Marco Gnavi, was able to visit as a religious counselor; and the resourceful Mario Marazziti was able to visit as a member of the press.

In November 1999, Mario attended a San Francisco conference of Americans working to end the death penalty. He had been invited to this conference by Sister Helen Prejean, the author of *Dead Man Walking*. There he met Sheila Murphy. Not long after—in June 2000—I met Sheila for the first time in the Basilica of Santa Maria in Trastevere. Sheila, a retired judge from Chicago, who is never to be found without some project in hand, had brought a class of Chicago law students with her to learn something about Roman law, ancient and modern. Of course, she would soon rope me into giving them all a tour of historic Rome—with an emphasis on legal aspects, please. That summer, just before she returned to the United States, she herself would be roped in: Mario would ask her to represent Dominique in his final appeals, for which the Community of Sant'Egidio had begun to collect contributions.

When we were introduced, Sheila Murphy put out her hand in a frank, comradely way, as if we were already old friends. She knew more of me than I of her. A few years older than I, she had grown up Irish Catholic in the self-congratulatory Protestant community of Colorado Springs and had suffered the taunts and disdain that accompany minority status in a hidebound town. She had read my book *How the Irish Saved Civilization* and felt it had finally justified her before that community of her childhood.

The handshake also told me that she believed herself the equal of any man but that she was a genial woman who got a kick out of male carryings-on, in other words a woman with a bunch of brothers. How can one gesture tell you so much about a stranger? It sometimes can, especially when the stranger has a lot of red hair piled on top of her head and a smile that is both open and crooked.

Despite her upbringing in the Rockies, Sheila speaks in an enviably credible Chicago accent, as if she'd been born in the Windy City and the winds themselves had flattened her vowels. Sheila is also a confessed alcoholic with a long history of success against addiction. One of the things I have come to admire most about her is her wanton openness on this subject. "Oh, you're a recovering alcoholic, too!" she will exclaim merrily to a fellow sufferer.

When the Community of Sant'Egidio invited her to represent Dominique in his final appeals, she signed on immediately. This would not be a cakewalk, not by any means. Before being called to the bench, Sheila had handled capital cases as a defense attorney, and none of her clients had ever been sentenced to death. But she was not a Texas lawyer, the commute between Chicago and Houston alone could do her in, she was supposed to be living in leisurely semiretirement. What on earth was she doing? she had to ask herself. She didn't really have an adequate answer to her own question.

So what. Sometimes there are things we have to go through, anyhow. Sheila forged ahead instinctively, as she often had in the course of her life. Where this would end she had no idea.

Then, in the fall of 2003, I had lunch with Sheila in Chicago while on a publicity tour for one of my books. Where was I going after Chicago, Sheila asked. I gave her my schedule, which ended in Houston not long before Christmas. "Then you can visit Dominique," she exclaimed. Book tours, which may sound glamorous to those who have never gone on one, are grueling exercises, a little like forced marches. I had already been out for many weeks and was looking forward to that last day in Houston, the return trip to my family in New York, and putting up my Christmas tree. Except for an unlikely accident—that the publicist who had arranged the tour was a Texan—I doubt Houston would have been on my schedule at all. Almost the last thing I wanted to do was visit a man on Death Row with whom I would have nothing in common. I foresaw an extra day in Houston and an embarrassing hour of trying vainly to find enough conversation.

But, looking across the table at Sheila's expectant face, I found I could not say no.

4

The first meeting between Dominique and Sheila Murphy
gave off no adumbrations of instant karma. Dominique, a
prisoner now for nearly eight years, had learned to be distrust-
ful of lawyers; and even this late-middle-aged one, a woman
whose sympathy is so effortlessly engaged that it seems to spill
from her like mother's milk, was going to have to work hard to
earn the confidence of this young convict, who had come to be
skeptical, even cynical, toward outsiders who came to visit
him. Many, both lawyers and sometime supporters,* had
come and gone by this point; many more had shown them-

---

* For simplicity's sake, I have omitted from this narrative some of the figures who
for a time assisted Dominique legally, as well as others who offered moral support.
In still other cases, I have mentioned such figures without elaborating much on
their roles.

selves to have their own self-serving agendas unconnected to Dominique's crying needs.

Dominique did exempt some repeat visitors from his silent scorn, especially occasional visitors from Rome, exotic to him at first, then gradually welcomed for their evident seriousness and solidarity with his suffering. And he had come to have positive feelings toward David Atwood, founder of the Texas Coalition to Abolish the Death Penalty, who turned up regularly, offering books and other simple services, and seemed unlikely to go away. Dave, a retired chemical engineer, has dedicated his retirement to the service of Death Row inmates, their families, and the families of their victims. He is an even-tempered, mild-mannered man but quietly unswerving, even relentless in his dedication. He would help bridge the gulf that yawned between Sheila's good heart and Dominique's distrust by insisting to Dominique on more than one occasion that this ebullient female judge with the Chicago accent was O.K.

Sheila first met Dominique in the summer of 2000 on her birthday, August 18. She was not his chief attorney, nor could she be; that role had been awarded to court-appointed lawyers Mike Charlton and Gary Taylor, who could not be removed from Dominique's case except by a judge's order. Sheila was initially surprised to find Dominique especially keen on retrieving the videotape that he assumed had been made automatically by the security camera of the store in front of which Andrew Lastrapes had been shot nearly eight years earlier.

Dominique understood that whatever had been videotaped that night had long since been taped over. But he had also read that it was possible to restore by electronic manipulation some semblance of the taped-over images. He had not been able to get Charlton and Taylor's investigator, nor the investigator who had preceded him, to look into the matter. However hopeless such a quest might have proved, Dominique's urgency proved to Sheila that, although Dominique was unwilling to rat on the real murderer, he was eager to let the evidence speak for itself.

Sheila, however, could find nothing: the store manager looked at her blankly and shrugged. No one worked there who had worked there in 1992; no one knew what had become of the old tapes; no one knew anything that could give Sheila the least help. She returned to Dominique empty-handed.

But gradually, almost without realizing that it was happening, Sheila overcame Dominique's suspicion of her by leaving the subject of his case and talking about her family, especially about her husband and her children, a son, Patrick, and a daughter, Brigid, both a little older than Dominique. It was an intuitive strategy, one that any law school would advise its students against: under no circumstances do you open your personal life to your clients! But Sheila, a refreshingly open woman, impelled to candor by her own temperament as well as by her experience of fighting her addiction, can talk about her family members almost as if they are there with her in the room. Dominique was fascinated and amazed: here was a mother who had an easy and natural relationship with her grown children, a mutually respectful relationship that knew no rigidity, no strictures, but was full of humor, elasticity, love, and . . . pleasure. To Dominique, the casual chat of this woman on the other side of the glass hit him with all the impact of a revelation.

Tentatively, Dominique began to ask Sheila questions— about how she talked to Brigid and Patrick and how they talked to her. Though only dimly realizing what she was doing at first, Sheila was holding up to Dominique a dream beyond all his imaginings: she was giving him a practical education in the nuts and bolts of healthy family life, a realm that lay outside anything in his experience. Finally, Sheila succeeded in closing the circle that was slowly uniting her and Dominique: she asked Dominique about his family. He told her briefly of the many horrors and of his concern for his brothers, but then he found himself concentrating on the paternal grandmother he had loved and lost—the one person who had always believed in him—and the immense loneliness that had overwhelmed his nine-year-old world when she died. That day, Sheila realized, Dominique was trying to keep her there, prolonging her visit with whatever conversational gambit he could come up with. His decision earlier in that visit to cross the line into his private suffering—to tell her about his grandmother—had sealed their new relationship.

Sheila found herself giving Dominique as much attention as she gave her own children, sending him postcards and phoning when she couldn't visit. Eventually, she asked her son to visit Dominique. Sheila would always think of that visit as miraculous: the on-duty staff unaccountably allowed Patrick to remain far beyond the customary hour, and in that time an irrevocable transformation occurred. By the end of the visit, Dominique and Patrick were calling each other "brother"—and they both meant it. Dominique now knew himself to be a member of a family, a family that wanted him.

There was another person whom Sheila was able to introduce to Dominique: her law clerk, Andrew Lofthouse, three years younger and three inches taller than Dominique, a middle-class, midwestern white boy with the rangy body of a tennis player (as opposed to Dominique's slightly squatter, more earthbound appearance), with whom Dominique could have expected to have little in common. Livingston was the first prison Andy ever found himself in—though he lacks the least hint of straight-laced rectitude and will refer obliquely to "my youthful indiscretions." It was precisely Andy's zany playfulness, the dance of lights in his eyes that says, "I'm not always a good boy," that appealed to Dominique, who possessed an obvious and irrepressible naughtiness of his own. Much of their bonding revolved around the usual male talk of sports and girls.

But if the predictable interests of men in their twenties helped the two to reach some common ground, Andy was perhaps the first person to get a fix on how intelligent Dominique was—and how manipulative he could be. "He figured this guy flew all the way down here, drove all the way up here, waited in line, this guy obviously wants to see me. It's just what people do to go on visits there. It's not easy to get to Livingston, Texas. And Dominique knew it and he had been having visits for eight or nine years by the time I got there; and so when I got there, I was one of a long line. And he knew how to manipulate every interview that he had. And he'd say in his letters, 'Well, I'm going to have a visit' or 'I need a visit,' and it was almost like his visits were his business meetings and he was the CEO. And I didn't recognize that until the second or third time I went down there. Because at first I thought he was desperate to meet me but the second or third time I went down I realized that the guy had a plan for this. These are his only outlets to an outside world. And I think Dominique over time certainly learned to trust me but I think he also respected me [because] I didn't really fall for a lot of his bullshit that a lot of the other visitors do."

By calling some of Dominique's initial bluffs, Andy was rewarded not only with Dominique's respect but with a mutual friendship that became deeply rewarding for both men. We can almost listen in on their evolving conversation:

"Why did you lie to me the first time?"

"Down here you don't know who you can trust, and I didn't know if I could trust you. I didn't want to invest everything in you if you were going to just walk away. I didn't want to get any false hope that people might really care about my case this time."

"Do you have much hope?"

"Hope is a loaded gun."

Dominique was full of such gnomic one-liners, allusive, mysterious, sometimes profound. He called Andy Confucius, a name he might have applied aptly to himself. But Andy-Confucius came gradually to realize that it was Dominique's nearly absolute isolation that had brought this street kid to an intellectual and psychological flowering that might otherwise never have happened. "He was very streetwise upon going in and he became book smart, intellectually smart after some time there. I think a lot of that had to do with his isolation from society stressors that had been in his life the whole time, specifically the street and his mother. When he finally was put not in the general population where non–Death Row [inmates are housed] but in a solitary cell, in a strange way that same cell that theoretically protected us from him also protected him from us. That's why he blossomed. And he would say that over and over to me, 'You know, being in here has made me the person I've always wanted to be.' "

Dominique Green, as removed from the world as any fourth-century Egyptian anchorite in his desert cell, was following an ancient path to spiritual enlightenment and personal transformation. Part of the formula, as had been the case for the desert fathers, was to look death straight in the eye. Andy suspected that Dominique "reconciled himself with the fact that they were going to kill him way before we even got involved in his case. He was on Death Row a long time, in which time they killed hundreds of people."

But there was far more to Dominique's spiritual quest than a confrontation with the probability of early death. "I think he realized that he wasn't going to be able to do everything that he wanted in his life because they were going to kill him. And yet he wanted to at least do something so his life had some kind of value. And I think that's why he forgave his mother and why he tried to help other people on Death Row. I think that's why he allowed himself to trust me and to trust Sheila. I mean, he used me and I don't blame him. His job was to get himself out of there. I used him to get out of some classes in law school! What I was amazed at was here is some guy down in a cell in Texas in the middle of nowhere and he's orchestrating a worldwide campaign that he started. He wrote letters to everybody. He's the one who contacted people. He orchestrated this campaign from his little cell and he has people all around the world working for him and thinking about him. And to me that's the most amazing thing about him. Granted, it was to save his own hide, but I found that amazing. Especially when you go down there and see that there are hundreds of people on Death Row in Texas and maybe four or five have what he had by the end of his life."

Indeed, a deepening familiarity with Dominique's case inspired the Community of Sant'Egidio to organize a worldwide movement to declare a moratorium on the use of the death penalty. As each new country signs on to this moratorium, the Roman Colosseum, ancient symbol of man's inhumanity to man, is lit up in celebration. In addition, the Community has initiated a worldwide Cities for Life program. In concert with the illumination of the Colosseum, 760 cities in fifty-six countries have followed suit, each lighting up a local monument on the occasion of a new state signatory.

Perhaps more important than this strikingly public effort, the Community has succeeded, working with other organizations (such as Amnesty International), in encouraging the

General Assembly of the United Nations to pass a resolution in favor of a moratorium. After the presentation by Sant'Egidio of more than five million signatures from 153 countries, all calling for a moratorium, the resolution passed the General Assembly on December 18, 2007, with 104 countries voting in favor, 54 against, among the latter China, Egypt, Saudi Arabia, Iran, and the United States of America. Since the passing of the resolution, additional countries have continued to sign on to this moratorium, either by legislative emendation or by outright abolition.

If Dominique was having an effect far beyond the immense gray walls of Livingston prison, there was also considerable drama taking place behind those walls, with Dominique as a principal player. Long before he began to reach out to his fellow prisoners, they reached out to him. Perhaps the most striking confirmation of this lies in the narrative Dominique wrote of his encounters with older inmates during his first years of imprisonment. This narrative was published, with Sheila's help, in the October 15, 2004, issue of *National Catholic Reporter*.

MORE THAN JUST A ROSARY

by Dominique Jerome Green

I really would enjoy it if one of the first things people noticed about me was the radiance of my smile. The conditions under which I live have robbed many here of the smallest traces of happiness that once could have been found at the very core of their being. So heads hanging down, faces plastered by frowns and defeatist attitudes are things you find here en masse. Which is why the simple fact that I can smile, I can laugh, I can allow myself not to take this seriously should be more than enough reason to capture folks' attention, but it's not.

Instead, people are drawn to the black and blue rosary that adorns my neck, which is made of 101 beads, and which hangs to below my waist. As long as it is, and as stand-outish as it is, I don't know why I thought very little attention would be paid to it. But whatever the case may be, that was definitely wishful thinking on my part, because everyone who sees me ends up asking me questions about the rosary. The questions have ranged from gang-related to religious, from natural curiousness to understanding, from playfully humorous to sarcastic.

I used to not answer the questions. If I responded, I used humor or wit to put an end to or deflect the questions.

The reason I wear the rosary and have kept it for all these years was personal, something that only belonged to me. But recently, even my attorney asked about it when she came to visit.

The time had come, I decided, to finally talk about the rosary.

When I first arrived on death row, I was just a kid—one confused, smart-mouthed and belligerent kid. Fortunately, back then death row was nothing like it is now. Now we are all individually isolated. Then the environment was communal. I could interact with men who saw in me the potential to grow. Those men taught me, they mentored me, they helped me find myself. They showed me how to open my eyes and in turn open up my mind.

Today it's not like that. The communal environment that enabled me to grow is denied men who come here today, men who need those teachers, those mentors and those spiritual guides to help them understand that coming here is not the end of their lives but merely a second chance.

That all sounds so easy now. But at first I couldn't accept or even fathom that concept. I was like, "How can you even call living here on Texas Death Row a second chance at life?" What finally allowed things to fall into perspective for me was when a friend, one of my mentors, was set to be executed.

He told me the fact that his number was being called and not mine was what would give me a second chance to use all the knowledge he had passed on to me to make a difference in someone's life. His words stuck to my heart.

With his passing, not only did I pick up his torch, but I also began making my rosary, bead by bead. Each bead represents a friend, mentor or spiritual guide of mine who has died and who gave me the chance to use their knowledge and wisdom to touch other lives.

I never expected my rosary to get so long. As messed up as the Texas judicial system is, I expected the courts or the people to eventually put a stop to what was going on down here.

But they haven't. And 11 years after I was sent here, the death toll continues to rise. More than 250 people have been executed since my arrival. I've known almost all of them. I chose to stop adding beads to my rosary at 101, because by then I understood how to use what I had learned to have an impact on the lives of others and to help make a difference.

Most men here will never get the chance to understand self-discipline from people like Paul Rougeau; how to have a sense of humor even when things are at their worst from people like Rick Jones; how to have whole countries believing in them and showing an outpouring of support to free them like Odel Barnes; how to be a friend and big brother like no other like Vincent Cooks; how to never let this place break one's mind, body or spirit like Emerson Rudd; how to lead by being a follower like Ponchai Wilkerson; how to make people change their beliefs in capital punishment as did the wrongfully executed Gary Graham; and how to look at being here as having a second chance at life like Da'woud.

Those are lives my rosary reflects. So no, it doesn't bother me that my smile is not and probably won't ever be the first thing people notice about me. After all, its radiance is allowed to come from what I wear around my neck anyway.

As any writer can attest, the straightforward simplicity of Dominique's prose is no simple matter. It is a hard-won achievement, made possible by vigilant exercises of mind and agonizing attention to writing skills. The mind's usually undifferentiated potpourri of half-thoughts and impressions must be sorted into clear and usable thoughts, which must then be expressed in a common English that readers can connect with. If we compare "More Than Just a Rosary" to Dominique's letter of June 13, 1995, to Stefania (pages 47–50), written more than nine years earlier, we encounter the same warm Dominique, but now possessed of a clarified eloquence and ability to communicate with others that come close to endowing his words with the impact of a professional writer. In Dominique we discover a true autodidact, who has used his desert cell as a school of self-improvement.

Dominique's solitary reflections also impelled him to provide more systematic assistance to his fellow inmates. Some of his attempts, such as the creation of football pools, may seem trivial, but only if you have never thought about what it would be like to live along Death Row. Dominique set up the football pools and bought off the guards so he could get his flyers passed around. Inmates would circle their favored teams, and each Monday Dominique would "announce" the winner and make sure the winner got everything that was coming to him. When you have little or nothing to look forward to, such an activity can reestablish some of the surprise and adventure of normal life. And beyond introducing the jump and thrill of the unknown, the football pool was a heroic attempt to create, as Andy Lofthouse saw it, "a sense of community there among the people on Death Row."

But far beyond football, Dominique spent much of his time helping his fellow inmates to understand the mysteries of Texas law. By diligent reading of the law books his supporters supplied him with, he had come to have an excellent grasp of his own case, which gave him the ability to enlighten others as to their real situation and its likely remedies. He understood both the probabilities and the occasional opening for a daring strategy, and he was constantly engaged in giving advice to others who were younger and less skilled than he.

Besides football pools and legal strategy, Dominique often endeavored to raise the spirits of his fellow inmates by an inventive variety of ploys. One of these was the creation of a sprawling manuscript, composed of contributions by prisoners. Given the immense obstacles to communication among the inmates, each living in solitary confinement, this manuscript, which now sits on my desk, typed by Dominique on the prison's barely functioning typewriter, is a considerable achievement.

In his foreword, Dominique stresses how conscious the contributors are that they must clear away "the racial prejudice that once divided us"; and the races of the contributors bear this out. One chapter of contributions is by Son Tran, a writer of Vietnamese origin, condemned to death at seventeen. His poetry is full of the dreamy mind games he plays to keep himself sane:

> In the dark
> I dance to a tune
> from a distant memory
> to ease the boredom
> of confinement
> to escape the walls
> of self-destruction
> to enjoy a moment
> of reprieve.
> Will you dance with me?

Another contributor is Tony Medina, of partly Mexican, partly European origin, who claims to be completely innocent of the crime of which he was convicted. With Dominique's help, however, he was able to get the attorney who had represented him disbarred (a first in a Texas capital case) and to force the court to grant him the right to a fresh appeal (another first).

A third contributor, Howard Guidry, an African American, writes with considerable pathos of the psychological effects of incarceration: "I try not to fall into routine. The bleakness of this place and the rigor of the rules and regulations produce a monotonous theme that many of the men here unconsciously fall into. I am always changing, rearranging the sparse furniture in my cage, working out sporadically, changing my sleeping hours. I alternate reading and writing depending on my mood. Typically I'll play a few games of chess at the end of most days. And I draw when my spirit moves me. . . . Here social interaction is strictly prohibited. I have not watched a television or played a game of dominoes in five years. We are isolated to one-man cages twenty-four hours each day. . . . The isolation experienced on Polunsky Unit today is of grave consequence to the human psyche. I have witnessed men literally lose their minds here."

At one point Guidry escaped, getting as far as the roof of the prison, and he considers this brief flight his most important accomplishment while in prison, because he was "climbing the roof of the prison, watching the stars and moon without looking at them through fence, glass or razor wire."

His description of what it is like for a prisoner to be told he has a visitor is heartrending:

> On occasion they let me out of my cage. An hour for recreation, some minutes to shower, a walk to disciplinary or some other institutional office. But it's rare that I fall out to visitation. [The walk to] the visitation room is the longest walk men experience on Death Row. That is, until the last walk. To me walking to visitation is like smoking indonesia. It starts in moments like this, while I'm writing: "Guidry, you have a visit. Get ready," says a picket control guard over the intercom. I put my pen down and take a deep breath; and then I'm high for the next six or seven hours. The escort guards have to take me out of the building that houses Death Row and into the open air in order to get me there. The outside walkway is lined on both sides with a hurricane fence and covered by a steel roof. I always try to count the steps from my cage to the visitation cage, but I always lose count the moment I step "outside." My senses are extraordinary for having been deprived. The subtle breeze against my skin, the scent of grassroots and freshly turned compost, the hypnotic vapor-blue sky, the earth's vibrations—nothing escapes me. The rhythm of my own feet against the concrete is the soundtrack to whatever fantasy I conjure up in a moment. The guards don't understand my silence. Silence is often a prelude to violence amongst a certain breed of men in prison. But my silence in these pseudo-serene walks is the silence of a child in awe.

It would be hard to overestimate how much comfort this manuscript gave to Dominique's fellow prisoners: they had created a book! Not only that, the dramatic increase in social cohesiveness—in a sense of belonging to a community of common experiences and common resolve—served as a powerful bane against the isolation of the cage. There are no mental health services offered to Death Row inmates. For whatever healing is done they themselves must be the healers. But as with all acts of generosity, the giver gets at least as much as he gives. In Andy Lofthouse's words, Dominique "was very much a big brother to a lot of [inmates], and I think that stemmed from his innate desire to just belong and have a family and have people who cared about him."

Dominique's own contribution to the manuscript is characteristic. Like the desert fathers, like the ancient Greek philosophers who carved the words "Know thyself" on the façade of their most sacred temple, he has similar advice to offer from the treasure trove of his own experience. He asks himself the question "If you were given the opportunity to say something to someone that would make a lasting impression on their life what would it be?" "The best answer to some of life's most difficult questions," he replies, "can always be found if you just stop and take a look in the mirror."

He describes the process by which he came to this self-knowledge:

One of the first things I learned in coming to Death Row was how to be myself. Simple as that may sound that was far from an easy task because before I came to Death Row I was many different things to many different people. As a result I went through a monumental identity crisis. I didn't know if I wanted to be a Muslim or a Christian religiously. I didn't know if I wanted to be a revolutionary or a gangster with my friends. I didn't know if I wanted to be a mack or a man when it came to women. I didn't know if I wanted to be a responsible leader or an easily influenced follower in regard to my life. I didn't know, after being condemned, if I should prove to the jury that sentenced me to die that I was not a monster. . . . I never had anyone in my life to teach me how to be me. That was something I had to take the time to discover on my own, and it was one hell of an experience.

It sounds almost as if he is grateful for the opportunity that prison has afforded him. But, steely realist that he is, he also has no illusion about the ambiguity of the gift he has been given:

My attorneys have filed a Writ of Certiorari on my behalf, which now sits before the United States Supreme Court. I have reached the final stage of my appeal and unfortunately don't expect to see next year.

Hope is indeed a loaded gun.

5

By this stage in his life, Dominique was even finding ways to have an impact on lives outside the prison. When Andy Lofthouse's oldest and best friend, a young journalist named Timothy Krahl, was killed in a snowboarding accident in Montana, where he had attended college, Andy, by his own account, "pretty much withdrew from everything for a while" and stopped visiting Dominique. Dominique, who would never go snowboarding, never attend college, never see Montana, could have been expected to view the accident as something with little relevance to him, even as an incident in a life he could only envy from afar. Rather, as Andy relates, "he sent me this card that said, 'I face death every day but it's nothing compared to losing someone who helps you appreciate life. Yet despite all the pain and suffering, you have something most people never will: wonderful, magical, and who knows how mischievous, memories. Those are the things that keep us alive in each other's hearts and can never die. Stay strong, my friend. Dominique Green.' " Andy was comforted and a little amazed by Dominique's words.

And Dominique succeeded in bringing the world into the prison. Not only did he now have international organizations working on behalf of himself and other inmates, he fiddled with an old radio till it brought in the sounds of major television stations, television itself being forbidden. By sharing this guerrilla technology with others, he was able to increase the inmates' understanding of the wider world. Nonetheless, as he admitted to Andy, "Mine gets more channels than anybody else's." Why, asked Andy, don't you just listen to the radio? "Man," replied Dominique, "with all the hillbilly shit they got around here? I can't listen to *that!*" There were limits to even Dominique's multicultural tolerance.

I have a letter from one of Dominique's fellow inmates, Ivan Cantu, a Mexican American confined for a while in the cell next to Dominique, that relates more exactly Dominique's effect on other prisoners. "His life," writes Ivan, "was like an open book and he never tried to hide anything. He just called it as he saw it, and this is why I think we got along so well. He shared stories of his good friend Sheila Murphy, his brother Hollingsworth, and his faith. One thing about Dominique is that he was respected by all who knew him. In prison, inmates tend to lean towards certain groups but not Stump, he did his own thing while always making sure people were cared for."

In Ivan's description we meet the achieved Dominique, Dominique the mature adult, Dominique the man he had always wanted to become. "I hope you don't mind," continues Ivan, "that I call him Stump, but really that's the name I knew him by. Actually it was Stumpa, but most called him Stump for short. He was always so kind, and if he couldn't actually help an inmate himself, he'd contact a friend or someone he knew who could help. Most of the time he kept his good deeds to himself, but one time another inmate needed a Hot Pot, and since Stump couldn't purchase it from his account"—an account to which outsiders may make donations for small purchases is maintained for each prisoner—"he asked a friend [on the outside] to assist with getting the inmate one. Obviously, Stump didn't have to do this, but he hated to see anyone suffer or do without. That's just the kind of person he was: he made sure people had what they needed or the right information to fight their case."

Glued to his radio during broadcasts of *60 Minutes*, *Face the Nation*, or his usual favorite, *Meet the Press* with Tim Russert, Dominique encouraged others to listen, too. For fellow prisoners, he served as a model of engagement with the world: "One thing I'll always remember is that he had a way with words, and he always tried to better himself—writing professors, studying law books, writing articles, studying vocabulary, even just spending time in prayer," writes Ivan. "He was truly a shining light to everyone he met. Inmates would actually forfeit their daily shower to recreate in his dayroom, so they could pick his brain."*

Ivan leaves us with this indelible picture of Dominique: "Even when his world was crashing, he always remained cool. And really, I don't think he was *trying* to be cool. He was just at peace." And like the peaceful Jesus of the gospels, Dominique was on the verge of an experience of transfiguration that would help carry him to his end.

"The most unlikely person, the most improbable situation— these are all 'transfigurable'—they can be turned into their glorious opposites." These are the words of Desmond Tutu, archbishop emeritus of Cape Town, South Africa, who won

---

* In addition to the Death Row prisoners' methods of communicating and sharing that I declined to describe in the Prologue, there is a further possibility occasionally open to them. Twice weekly each inmate who is deemed to be cooperative and deferential is permitted his hour of exercise "outside"—that is, in a small dayroom or recreation yard composed of cement walls, a cement floor, and a ceiling made of bars. The spaces between the bars of this ceiling, however, are open to the outside, which means that the prisoner can "feel the sun and on occasion feel the breeze if one happens to come through that particular day," as Ivan Cantu has described it to me. Running the length of the room is a divider made of bars and mesh. One prisoner exercises on one side of this divider, a second prisoner on the other side. This arrangement allows some communication between two prisoners, but arranging to meet a particular prisoner in this way requires considerable prior planning and the cooperation of a guard. Normally, a prisoner is allowed to "go outside" only with another prisoner housed in the same section. But arranging to exercise with a particular prisoner is sometimes possible if one can bribe a guard by forfeiting something else, such as a shower—a principal daily pleasure. Though each Death Row prisoner has the right to a daily shower, this can be taken only in the presence of a guard, and the guards are particularly averse to spending their time in this way.

the Nobel Peace Prize in 1984 for his many years of sublimely courageous work in the struggle against the apartheid of his then white-ruled homeland. A few months after I first went to Livingston, Tutu was about to visit Dominique, a visit that would be surrounded by as much hubbub and media attention as Dominique could ever have hoped for.

"The Arch," as Tutu is called by many of his many friends, was coming to the United States on a speaking tour in March 2004. I had been his publisher at Doubleday during the previous decade, and over the course of that time he and I had become friends. I was also a friend of his literary agent, Lynn Franklin, a woman of considerable sympathy for others. She shared with me the details of the schedule for Tutu's speaking tour. He had one day off during his tour, March 24. Even more serendipitous, on March 23 he would speak in Oklahoma City; on March 25 he was due in Dallas. So—at least theoretically—it would be possible for him to fly from Oklahoma City to Houston on March 24, meet with Dominique, and then fly on to his appointment in Dallas.

The obstacles to such a plan were considerable: in order to keep him on schedule, I would need to arrange for private planes and chauffeured cars. And somehow I would have to get him to agree to go far out of his way to meet a man he'd never heard of, causing considerable disruption to his schedule. I would also need to secure the cooperation of his lecture agency, a brusquely efficient organization not especially known for its devotion to causes unconnected to their bottom line.

But the most daunting objection to this emerging scheme

lay in my knowledge of Desmond Tutu's delicate health: he had prostate cancer and had recently undergone treatments that left him less vigorous than usual; moreover, he had struggled his whole life against the effects on his body of diseases he had contracted in childhood, tuberculosis and polio. The polio, in particular, had left his right side weak, to such an extent that he had a soft handshake and, when tired, a pronounced limp. He would soon turn seventy-three. As if all this did not speak against my plan, there was the archbishop himself, a man who craves the oasis of silence, meditation, and prayer the way others crave human society. I knew he would be depending on the one day he had off to restore his spiritual equilibrium.

Well, I reasoned, if anyone I know is a grown-up, capable of making his own decisions and saying no to what he knows is beyond his strength, it is Desmond Tutu. So I would send him an e-mail message, telling him of Dominique's situation and Dominique's love of his writings, particularly *No Future Without Forgiveness*, and of the effect of that book—through Dominique's instrumentality—on the inhabitants of Texas Death Row. It would then be up to the man himself to decide whether or not to attempt a visit.

I sent my e-mail. Lynn Franklin kindly sent another, supporting mine. We each received an identical return e-mail from the Arch, which began: "I don't know why I ever allowed myself to get mixed up with people like you." Reading that first sentence, I knew he would come.

I will not bore you with the obstacles that had to be overcome to make the hoped-for visit a reality. Sheila Murphy and I pulled out all the stops and called in all our chits. One by one, obstacles fell away, not least the recalcitrance of the lecture agency when my contact there realized that her cherished godmother and I were old friends. On the dismal gray morning of March 24, I found myself in a chauffeur-driven limo, approaching a tiny airstrip in the middle of the Texas woods, where a private plane, belonging to the wealthy friends of a New Hampshire lawyer, was soon to land, disgorging the Most Reverend Desmond M. Tutu in his battered old cap and undistinguished traveling costume.

As we sped through those woods on our way to Livingston, the archbishop silently reciting his morning prayers and working his way through the long list of those he prays for daily, I was aware of our vulnerability. For weeks beforehand, the impending visit was news in all the Texas papers. Here we were—Desmond Tutu and his iconoclastic assistant Travis, the driver and I—traveling through this lonely forest, a second long black limo behind us, easy targets for assassination by any hothead, racist, or wacko who wished to take a shot at us. Though I had formally requested protection, I had been sent a message by the local police that they were simply too busy to provide any.

Now that Tutu had landed, I had another request to make of him. After he visited Dominique, there was to be a press conference, to which he had already given his approval. It would be hosted by St. Luke's, the small Episcopal church in Livingston. The congregants, extremely excited that such a famous Anglican churchman was to grace them with his presence (the Episcopal Church being the U.S. province of the worldwide Anglican Communion), were planning an elaborate welcome. The ladies of the church, who had been cooking up a storm, would graciously provide lunch not only for the archbishop but for all the local, national, and international press. I had told the church representatives that, as we were in the midst of Lent, the archbishop would not be taking lunch but would be fasting. No matter, they were forging ahead with their culinary plans.

The rector and the warden of the church would be there to greet the archbishop on his arrival and would press him to celebrate eucharist after the press conference. I had hoped, rather, that my friend would have some time to rest once the press conference was over. But I had been unable to dissuade the churchpeople from their resolve to invite him to preside at their eucharist before returning to the airstrip and the private plane that would be waiting for him. Knowing that they would ask him, I thought it best to warn him of their intention and thus give him time to compose his regrets. Of course, he replied, he would accept their invitation to preside at the eucharist. And that was that.

We arrived at the prison without incident and were ushered into the office of the prison warden, where we were greeted with exaggerated courtesy by the prison's officials and the archbishop somehow managed to take an interest in each person he was introduced to. Then, at last, he and I were waiting while Dominique was brought in shackles from his cell to the visitors' gallery. As I described in the Prologue, the visitor waits in a tiny cubicle facing a window of thick double glass. On his side is a telephone receiver. On the other side of the double glass is an answering receiver. Through these handsets, visitor and prisoner converse with each other. The prisoner's shackles binding his wrists behind his back are unlocked only after he is seated on his side of the glass, the door behind him has been bolted, and he has put his hands and wrists through a slot in the door, where a guard with a key is waiting. The shackles on his ankles are not removed. Everything seems done for maximum awkwardness and humiliation.*

While setting up the terms of this visit, I had begged the prison authorities to allow a sacramental visit. What is that, they wanted to know. The archbishop, I replied, would like to bless the prisoner. To do this in the most effective way, he wishes to place his hands on the prisoner's head. To be truthful, I was not so much interested in achieving this result for the sake of the blessing itself. After all, a priest (or anyone, for that matter) can bless another through two sheets of glass— or across half a world, if necessary. It is the intention, not the proximity, that makes the blessing.

Dominique, like all Death Row prisoners of the State of Texas, was kept in solitary confinement and never touched by

---

* Sheila Murphy has taken particular note of these circumstances as they affect the children of Death Row inmates: "No place for children to play, no books, no coloring books. They just have to sit and wait while their mother talks on the phone to their father. They just look on with eyes so sad—such inhumanity to innocent children under color of law."

anyone. How horrible, I often thought, to be so confined as never to feel a human touch, except by way of coercion or humiliation. But the prison authorities would make no allowance for a sacramental visit, not even by a religious figure as famous and revered as Desmond Tutu. What if a prisoner wished to be baptized, I asked. Would you deny him that? No, came the even response, we do allow that—on the night before execution.

Since it is impossible to shake hands through panes of glass, the custom is for the prisoner to place his right hand, palm out, on his side of the glass, while his visitor, mimicking the prisoner's action, places his own right hand against the glass on his side—as close as the two can come to touching, though each touches only the cold rigidity of glass. As Dominique positioned his fire-scarred right hand against the glass, Desmond Tutu raised his own polio-weakened hand in response.

I left them to have their own private meeting, which was no doubt exceedingly sacramental and full of blessings. Sheila Murphy and I waited in an adjoining room, where after the first few minutes we could hear repeated peals of laughter from both men. As their visit proceeded through its hour and a half, joy continued to break out, sometimes uproariously. They were getting along just fine, as I knew they would, if more hilariously than anyone could have anticipated.

In the end, Tutu gave Dominique an inscribed copy of *An African Prayer Book*, the archbishop's own anthology of intensely beautiful African prayers from pharaonic times to the present, collected from virtually every African religious tradition, a project I had suggested to him. Published by Doubleday in 1995, it has remained in print ever since. I mention it here because I believe its texts give off sparks of the eclectic, playful, and profound humanity of the conversation that took place that day. For those who would come closer to the deep meaning of this encounter between a monumental man and a Death Row inmate, the spirit of that day may still be sought in the pages of *An African Prayer Book*.

Like Jesus in his transfiguration, his secret encounter on the mountain with Moses and Elijah, those great figures of ancient Hebrew tradition, witnessed dimly by three of his earthbound disciples, Dominique in his meeting with Desmond found confirmation and exaltation—and strength to move forward to his appointed end.

As we exited the prison, Desmond, Sheila, and I were confronted by interviewers and camera crews from local television stations. When we reached St. Luke's, we found hundreds of reporters, as well as many church members, waiting for us. Somehow, the police who could not protect the archbishop earlier managed to be on hand for crowd control. What the archbishop had to say of Dominique was simple and eloquent. Over and over he repeated—on this day and in the days to come—that Dominique "is a remarkable advertisement for God." Privately he reassured me that I had not been "hyperbolic" in my description of Dominique and that he had been "greatly enriched" by the encounter.

"I was very humbled to be in his presence," said Tutu at the news conference in that sweet, hushed, but commanding voice of his, "because I felt I was in the presence of God. This is not the monster that many would expect or think, but a human being, a human being who has grown. He's like a flower opening and you see the petals come up, particularly when you see him speaking about his concern for others. He wasn't self-pitying. I'm glad I came. I come away deeply enriched from my encounter with an extraordinary man. He is a remarkable young man and it would be one of the greatest tragedies if someone like Dominique were executed." He made a point of describing the rosary Dominique wears around his neck and its meaning. Many reporters found this particularly fascinating and used it in their stories.

Of the death penalty he said that it is "not a deterrent. I think it is an obscenity that brutalizes. As a believer, [I find it] the ultimate giving up, because our faith is a faith of ever-new beginnings. [If] you execute them, you say, 'I close the possibility of them ever being able to repent and to change.'"

Of the prison he said, "Dominique spends twenty-three hours of a day in solitary confinement, with one hour for exercise, alone. Now that is torture. The punishment begins the moment you come into Death Row. The deprivation—can you imagine not being able to be touched? We did a high-five through the glass as it was, anyway."

Of the prison guards and officials he said, "They were some lovely people, but I just wonder what effect working in that environment can have on people. It's so destroying—for everyone there."

He spoke of his conversation with Bernatte Lastrapes, the widow of the victim: "She said she is pissed off. Those are her lady-like words. She is pissed off because the white accomplice got off scot-free. That really has riled her and she thinks the other three should have the opportunity to begin again. She doesn't want Dominique Green executed. I hope we can correct what has been a gross miscarriage of justice."

He spoke of the paradox of the American character: "You are a very generous people, Americans, and it is very difficult to square with your remarkable vindictiveness, which doesn't square with your remarkable generosity. [Dominique] has already been in jail eleven years. That's a huge slice of someone's life. I hope the attention will make other people involved so that it becomes a groundswell and people know this is not what we should be doing. Don't dehumanize yourselves as a society by carrying out the death penalty!"

Having done all he could do with words, Desmond Tutu turned to sacrament. He celebrated mass in a packed church, choosing in his sermon not to dwell on the subject of the press conference but on the feast of the day, Annunciation Eve, celebrating the encounter of Mary of Nazareth with Gabriel, the messenger from God who invited her to become the mother of Jesus Christ. He imagined Mary saying no: " 'What? Me!! In this village you can't even scratch yourself without everybody knowing about it! You want me to be an unmarried mother? I'm a decent girl, you know. Sorry, try next door.'

"If she had said that, we would have been up a creek. Mercifully, marvelously, Mary said, 'Behold the handmaid of the Lord; be it unto me according to thy word,' and the universe breathed a cosmic sigh of relief, because she made it possible for our Savior to be born.

"Mary was a poor teenage girl in Galilee and reminds us that transfiguration of our world comes from even the most unlikely places and people. You, the people of Livingston, Texas, are the indispensable agents of change. You should not be daunted by the magnitude of the task before you. Your contribution can inspire others, embolden others who are timid, to stand up for the truth in the midst of a welter of distortion, propaganda, and deceit; stand up for human rights where these are being violated with impunity; stand up for justice, freedom, and love where they are trampled underfoot by injustice, oppression, hatred, and harsh cruelty; stand up for human dignity and decency at times when these are in desperately short supply. God calls on us to be his partners to work for a new kind of society where people count."

When mass was ended, Desmond Tutu stood at the church door and greeted each worshipper individually, shaking hands, embracing, somehow finding the right word for each of these encounters with strangers. By now, I could see, he was exhausted and his right hand and right side were giving him trouble. After he had unvested and resumed his street clothes, I was determined to get him into that limo and on his way as fast as possible.

He emerged from the sacristy and took in the scene, refusing to be hurried toward his car. There, beyond the crowds of people who could not bring themselves to leave, beyond the rolling lawn of the church's property was a ring of uniformed police, beefy white men with crossed arms and reflective sunglasses, the only people Desmond Tutu had not yet greeted. With his customary smile hiding his grim determination, he forced himself to limp down the driveway to the edge of the road, where the cops stood, towering over his tiny figure. Though only five feet four inches tall, Tutu seemed at that moment to be shrinking to an even more diminutive size. Nevertheless, he shook the hand of each astonished policeman and thanked them, every one. Then he was ready to go.

After the limo had taken off, Dave Atwood of the Texas Coalition to Abolish the Death Penalty murmured to no one in particular, perhaps to the now bright air in the glow of the afternoon sun, "Livingston will never be the same." The visit suffused Dominique and his fellow Death Row prisoners with fresh optimism. They knew perfectly well that all the forces that were ranged against them were still in place, but they now had the best champion they could ever have conjured up and he had brought the world to Livingston as witness to their pain. One prisoner, Kenneth Foster Jr.,* expressed his enthusiasm in a poem entitled "The Anointing":

---

* Kenneth Foster was on Death Row when he wrote his poem. He had been sentenced under Texas's infamous "law of parties" for innocently driving a car from which a man disembarked and killed another man. Thanks to the heroic efforts of the appellate lawyer Keith Hampton, Sheila Murphy, and Andrew Lofthouse, his sentence has recently been commuted to life in prison.

Three cheers for Tutu,
the Catholic Zulu,
our black pope,
who smiled upon Death Row
and left tears as
spiritual libation
for dried souls to grow on.
Go on wit' yo' bad self, Desmond,
testing the morals of South Africa and
the dirty south,
trekking through the paths of
Black Death,
breathing
Green Life
for all willing
to be blessed with a
Holy Kiss
by lips that know how to speak a
Peace Beyond Understanding.
We stood hand in hand with you,
and still do,
hoping to remain the prayer in your heart
that asks for forgiveness of our souls
in a land barren of mercy,
bearing our crosses,
buried in the steel of
Texas Death Row!

Despite the buoyant optimism we all felt that day, the possibility of success against the machinery of Texas "justice" remained minuscule. The story of Desmond Tutu's visit was picked up by media throughout the country and beyond, but it was all a momentary wonder; within a day or two, the country and the world had many other things to think about. In a foreshadowing of what was to come, I noted that not a few published reports were garbled, incomplete, even malicious. Tutu had talked at length about his telephone conversation with the widow of the victim, though, as he explained, he had been unable to meet with her because she had just been hospitalized. There was no report of this in the *Houston Chronicle*, however, merely a quote from Diane Clements, president of an organization called Justice for All. "I guess Desmond Tutu forgot to visit the family of Andrew Lastrapes," asserted Clements ignorantly. Later, I learned that the reporter had included an account of Tutu's conversation with Bernatte Lastrapes in her story but that it had been excised by an editorial pencil and the quote from Clements set in its place. In other press accounts, Clements and others dismissed Tutu's visit to Livingston by claiming it was only in aid of his promoting his latest book, *God Has a Dream*—which he may have promoted on his speaking tour but which was never mentioned the entire time he spent in Livingston.

In fact, prior to the archbishop's visit Sheila Murphy and Dave Atwood had been trying for some time to locate Bernatte Lastrapes. Once they had found her and were able to connect her with Tutu, they were also able to make contact with her sons. Two of these, Andrew and Andre, who had been twelve and ten respectively when their father was killed, began to visit Dominique. Soon the three men, all of the same generation, all black Houstonians who had grown up in straitened circumstances, were fast friends. But Dominique could no longer wear his rosary when he met visitors. A new rule just happened to forbid the wearing of rosaries, which were now seen as "security threats." In a letter to me, Dominique wondered, "Are they actually labeling God as a security threat?"

In my response, I took some time to give Dominique a sense of who I believed he was and at the same time to offer him the sort of literary discourse I knew he craved:

You have, I'm sure, had to put up with petty harassments of this sort for years. When people have unlimited power over others, we know they will be tempted to abuse that power. Some men and women are even drawn to professions that will give them such power: there are not a few teachers, clergy, nurses, police, prosecutors, who take the jobs they take because of the enormous license these jobs give them to abuse other human beings. And if such is true of these common professions, how much truer it must be of the unusual profession of prison guard. Psychology of course tells us that it is the abused who end up as abusers, it is those who have been beaten who wish to beat, those who have been belittled who wish to belittle, those whose souls have been destroyed who need to destroy the souls of others. You must have figured this out a long time ago; and I'm sure you know that these psychological traits are not so fated or predetermined that the afflicted person can do nothing to change himself. The abused does not have to become an abuser. He can reflect on his history, come to see it for what it is, and make the decision not to repeat history, not to do to others what was done to him. That is always an immensely courageous decision, one that requires the bravery to look squarely at one's own history and name it accurately, then the courage to rein in one's own evil tendencies. It takes a mind and a heart working together—rather than rigidly separated from each other, even unknown to each other as so many people's minds and hearts are.

No one survives childhood without some such scars. The English poet Philip Larkin has a funny poem on the subject, called "This Be the Verse":

They fuck you up, your mum and dad.
    They may not mean to, but they do.
They fill you with the faults they had
    And add some extra, just for you.

But they were fucked up in their turn
    By fools in old-style hats and coats,
Who half the time were soppy-stern
    And half at one another's throats.

Man hands on misery to man.
    It deepens like a coastal shelf.

> Get out as early as you can,
>   And don't have any kids yourself.

For my money, the poem misses greatness because in the last stanza the poet loses his nerve. Yes, he makes us laugh, but he also wants us to despair as he despairs—to agree with him that our condition is so hopeless that the obliteration of the human race would be preferable to the continued reproduction of new human beings—that this would be the best outcome we could "hope" for, which would actually entail the death of any kind of real hope. This is true cynicism, which I'm sure you have had to endure a great deal of.

I prefer the solution of a poet like the nineteenth-century priest Gerard Manley Hopkins, who is sensitive to the terrible tragedies that human beings inflict on one another, so sympathetic that his pain on behalf of others is sometimes the realest, most physical element in his poems. He has a poem called "Brothers" in which he sits watching a school play. Next to him is a boy whose younger brother is acting in the play, and Hopkins feels all the older brother's anxiety on behalf of his younger sibling, his hope for his brother. He doesn't bother to tell us whether the younger boy performed well or not. His only point is the older brother's sympathetic suffering. The poem ends:

> Ah Nature, framed in fault,
> There's comfort then, there's salt;
> Nature, bad, base, and blind,

Dearly thou canst be kind;
There dearly then, dearly,
I'll cry thou canst be kind.

It's almost an answer to Larkin, even though it was written a century earlier. Hopkins doesn't deny how horrible human beings can be to one another; in fact, he acknowledges it ("bad, base, and blind"). But he points out another phenomenon, the reality of human sympathy, which in the end is the only thing that can redeem us from Larkin's (or anyone else's) despair.

To be hopeful is to be courageous. You certainly can't be hopeful without courage because each day is fraught with examples of what Larkin is talking about. To be hopeful is to steel ourselves against all the obvious and easy reasons to despair and, instead, to *choose* to hope.

I hope none of this sounds like I'm lecturing you. I'm just trying to give you some idea of who I think you are and why I have such admiration for you. The easy thing (always, everywhere) is to despair, to give up; the hard thing, the thing that takes interior, invisible strength, is to hope. In this business, I'm sure you could teach me much more than I could teach you. . . .

As I say to my own children (who are at such a distance, one in California, the other in the Czech Republic, both about your age): a big hug.

Love,
Tom

In a letter of mid-April to Marco Gnavi, the Sant'Egidio priest, Dominique, despite the misgivings that he kept mostly to himself, continued to express high hopes for a positive outcome to his case: "Tomorrow some reporter from South Africa is coming over to see me. Who knows just what all this will grow into? My hope is that the attention will continue to increase until enough is generated that I will have a platform to save my life." But Texas was deaf to any music but its own; and Sheila Murphy's legal advocacy had begun too late to have any but a marginal effect on Dominique's chances.

Dominique's legal team had filed a second habeas corpus petition, this one in federal court, but in February 2002, the U.S. District Court dismissed it and denied a certificate of appealability. In October 2003, the U.S. 5th Circuit Court of Appeals denied Dominique's request to appeal the U.S. District Court's denial of the federal habeas petition. In February 2004, Dominique petitioned the U.S. Supreme Court for the second time for a writ of certiorari, which, if granted, would initiate a Supreme Court review of the lower court's decision in Dominique's case. That June, however, at a hearing in the Harris County Courthouse, Dominique was given his death date—October 26—even though the Supreme Court had yet to rule. (Sheila and many others suspected that Harris County officials were determined to execute him prior to election day 2004, because the Harris County district attorney, Chuck Rosenthal, was running for reelection against a quasi-anti-death-penalty black candidate and the insiders didn't want Rosenthal's run clouded by this unresolved case.)

This was the one time that Sheila was able to touch Dominique because his guards allowed her to meet with him briefly at the courthouse after he was given his date. She put her arm around him with the easy familiarity she would display toward one of her own adult children. But when the Supreme Court denied Dominique's petition on October 4, 2004, the feast of Saint Francis of Assisi, Dominique's fate was sealed.

A tremendous amount of work had gone into these petitions on the part of Sheila and other lawyers she had managed to attract to Dominique's cause. And like the good mother she is, Sheila was not giving up. She sent out pleas to all the members of the Texas Board of Pardons and Paroles, she got others to do likewise, she sent a plea to Governor Rick Perry and got others to do so as well. (Among the many letter writers were a number of distinguished American jurists, Archbishop Tutu, and Joseph Fiorenza, the Roman Catholic bishop, soon to be archbishop, of Galveston-Houston.) She helped organize a press conference, featuring the Lastrapes brothers, who issued a public plea that Dominique's life be spared. In the end, it was all for naught.

Though one member of the Board of Pardons and Paroles actually voted to commute Dominique's sentence, it was hardly enough; and it is doubtful that his fellow members even took the time to examine the wealth of materials that Sheila sent them, which included a video of Bernatte Lastrapes begging for Dominique's life. "All of us," said Bernatte, "have forgiven Dominique for what happened and want to give him another chance at life. Everyone deserves another chance." Countering this impressive plea, state prosecutors informed the board members that Dominique had killed two white men, something entirely fictional. Sheila could not persuade Dominique's principal attorneys to contradict this fiction or to request that the board members visit Dominique, something only lawyers licensed in Texas were in a position to do.

It was well known that Perry, who had succeeded George W. Bush as governor, meant to end his tenure with more executions to his name than the amazing number racked up by his predecessor. He has more or less succeeded: whereas Bush presided over 152 executions in six years, Perry will have presided over at least 186 by the end of 2008, though he still lags somewhat behind Bush's numbers on a per-year basis.

With enviable confidence in his own righteousness and that of his state (and startling contempt for the judgment of others), Perry, through a spokesman, has recently responded to the appeal of the European Union that Texas enact a moratorium on the death penalty: "230 years ago, our forefathers fought a war to throw off the yoke of a European monarch and gain the freedom of self-determination. Texans long ago decided that the death penalty is a just and appropriate punishment for the most horrible crimes committed against our citizens. While we respect our friends in Europe, welcome their investment in our state and appreciate their interest in our laws, Texans are doing just fine governing Texas." No country may join the European Union if it countenances the death penalty, and more and more countries beyond Europe have been abandoning the practice. The United States consistently ranks fourth among countries still employing the practice, outranked in the number of executions only by China, Iran, and Saudi Arabia, those bastions of antimonarchical freedom.

The proximity of the execution date began to weigh on Dominique with such force that he was no longer able to collect his thoughts or maintain his usual cool, any more than Jesus could while contemplating his approaching death in the garden of Gethsemane. As Dominique wrote to Archbishop Tutu in early September:

> I am doing as well as one probably could expect, thanks largely to the overwhelming abundance of love and support heaped upon me in massive amounts these past few weeks. Strong-willed and thick-skinned as I may be, things have been a lot harder on me than I imagined. Because aside from having to face an execution date myself, I am having to endure it with some close and dear friends.
>
> On August the 26th, I lost one of them. His name was James Vernon Allridge III. I had known him for the past 8 years. He was a model prisoner. A positive influence. And one of the few perfect examples found here of what it means—meant—to be rehabilitated. Sadly, none of that was allowed to matter, despite all that he'd done, accomplished and achieved.
>
> It had been a while since someone that I was close to was

executed. So his execution crushed me a little bit. For the past $2^1/_2$ weeks my concentration hasn't been the same. It's been extremely difficult for me to find my focus and undertake even some of the smallest things.

I have been trying to write this letter to you for the last week and a half. Usually, at times like this (when I am going through a lot) I find a way to excel. But after losing James and facing the upcoming execution date (October 5th) of the best friend life could ever give me—a person I've known since I was fourteen—who in coming here not only grew up with me but helped to change the entire dynamics of Texas Death Row, named Edward Green III [no relative], my nerves have been stripped raw and, contrary to my outward appearance, I am walking the line of breaking down and mentally, physically, and spiritually crumbling.

Dominique was dealing with a syndrome that has often been noted by sympathetic observers: each fresh execution engenders traumatic distress in the remaining inhabitants of Death Row.

As the steps toward his own execution moved inexorably forward, Sheila Murphy kept up her drumbeat of interventions. I was not in Texas but in Europe, on a long planned trip to visit my son in Prague, after which I was to do some necessary research in Italy, Germany, France, and England for a book on the Middle Ages that I was writing. I remained in regular contact with Sheila's Chicago office and with Sheila's wonderful assistant, Kathryn Gough. I knew of Sheila's hopes for a last-minute reprieve, and I was more aware than I wished to be of their unlikelihood. In Prague I decided that I must send Dominique a letter. But what kind of letter do you write to someone about to die?

Dearest Dominique,

I'm so sorry to be traveling this week so far from you, but it could not be helped. I have no crystal ball and have no better idea of what will happen next than anyone else. But I am full of pain on your behalf. If all goes well (or at least as well as we could possibly hope), I will greatly look forward to seeing you after I return from Europe. If all goes as badly as possible . . . I will look forward to seeing you when we all meet merrily in heaven. What is important about a life is not its length but its intensity and direction. Yours is full of intensity, and your direction is so admirable that few could equal you, certainly not I.

Here is a prayer from the Book of Wisdom, which was written in Greek by an unknown writer who lived in North Africa in the century before Jesus. It is usually translated a little stiffly, so I have made my own translation. I hope it may be a help to you, whatever the outcome may be.

The souls of the just are in the hands of God,
And the torments wrought by evildoers
Can never touch them again.
It is true that they appeared to die—
But only in the eyes of people who cannot see

And who imagined that their passing away was a defeat,
That their leaving us was an annihilation.
No, they are at peace.
If, as it seemed to us, they suffered punishment,
their hope was rich with immortality;
slight was their correction, great will their blessings be.
God was putting them to the test,
And has proved them worthy to be with him;
He has tested them like gold in a crucible,
And accepted them as a perfect holocaust.
In the hour of judgment they will shine in glory,
And will sweep over the world like sparks through stubble.
They will judge nations, rule over peoples,
And the Lord will be their king forever.
Those who trust in him will come to understand the truth,
Those who are faithful will live with him in love.
Only grace and mercy await them—
All those whom God, in his compassion, has called to
    himself.

Thank you for your gracious friendship, Dominique. I
think of you often, pray for you always, and will never forget
you.

Much love,
Tom

Sheila Murphy was able to read this to Dominique on the
day before his execution. He asked her to read it through a

second time; and then he took it with him to his cell for a third reading, so I believe I did manage—typing in my son's studio in faraway Prague—to find the right words, however cold the comfort such a belief confers.

Dominique's last day was filled with drama. Almost at the last moment, Sheila and Andy Lofthouse were able to locate Jessica Tanksley, who happened to be visiting her family in Houston. Still startlingly beautiful (as Andy in particular could not help but notice), Jessica was now a self-possessed, much traveled, multilingual young woman soon to be awarded her medical degree from the Universidad Iberoamericana in Santo Domingo, Dominican Republic. Though she and Dominique had been out of touch for years, she came immediately to the prison, still unmarried, still (as was patently obvious to all) in love with Dominique. By then, Dominique's mother, Stephanie, was there as well. Dominique had asked Sheila to leave Stephanie out of the loop so that she could not disrupt things and draw all attention to herself, as he was sure she would attempt to do. But Sheila decided to disregard Dominique's wishes in this one matter, "because," she said later, "if there's one moment tomorrow that he wishes his mother were here, then I've blown it."

So Dominique had a final meeting with his mother, but one that also involved Sheila: "He motioned for me to come over and he said, 'Sheila, would you sit with my mom and me for just a few minutes? It's really important to me because she and I have had very poor parenting and she doesn't know how.

Would you help her learn to pattern as a parent should, teach her how to do it?' And I said, 'Well, how would I do that?' And he said, 'Well, just talk to me like you always do. We'll just talk, and you listen, Mom. So you can do it with my brothers.' And so we talked like we always did, you know, we joked and all."

Then Sheila told Stephanie that Jessica was waiting her turn. "You were once young," said Sheila, "and so was I, and we can remember how we loved seeing the person we loved when we were young, and Jessica is here and Dominique hasn't had much time with her these last ten years, so why don't we give our place to Jessica?" Miraculously, Stephanie agreed. The two older women moved off and allowed Jessica to speak privately with Dominique.

Jessica saw that the discreet beauty she had recognized long ago in her first meeting with Dominique had blossomed exponentially. His was now a presence that overcame any other energy in the room. She promised him that she would always, always remember him, and he said that for him that would be enough.

Later, when only the law team remained, Dominique began to call Sheila "Mom." It wasn't a slip of the tongue, as Sheila realized: the first time he did it, he winked at her. Andy also had a last conversation with his friend, who had refused to order a last meal. Like his model Desmond Tutu, he was fasting. What, Andy asked, would you eat if you decided to have a last meal? "Jessica," came the smiling reply. It seemed as if, on this last day, Dominique had worked his way free of the spiritual crumbling he had written about to Archbishop Tutu. He was back in his usual groove, calling the shots and playfully pushing these final encounters to heightened significance.

But now it was almost time for Dominique to be taken from the Livingston prison to the Huntsville Death House. Dominique spent his last few minutes in his cell dividing up his meager possessions for his friends. Andy got all his legal notes. In the weeks ahead, as Andy read through the notes, he came to the firm conclusion that Dominique had trained himself like a law student in every legal subtlety and strategy and had succeeded in being the best lawyer of them all. To the Lastrapes brothers, Dominique gave his inscribed copy of *An African Prayer Book* and his rosary. He also directed that the payment from *National Catholic Reporter* for his essay on his rosary, the only legitimate earnings he had ever made, be given to the Lastrapes family. Everyone received an appropriate gift.

Two guards arrived to take Dominique, but deferred their mission for a few minutes at Sheila's urging, so that everyone, especially Jessica, could say a last good-bye. Sheila could see the pain in the eyes of the guards and recalled the archbishop's speculation about what this business did to the spirits of those whose work is death. Then, as the guards escorted Dominique along a glass-enclosed corridor, Sheila and Andre Lastrapes were able to accompany him for some distance on the other side of the glass. Soon enough, the two parties—Dominique and his guards, Sheila and the other friends of Dominique— were on their way in separate vehicles through the pretty Texas countryside to Huntsville.

Huntsville, a cheerful, outwardly gracious community, has to be one of the strangest human settlements on the surface of the earth, a town organized around its Death House. So many in the town work for the Huntsville prison or for one of the six other prisons in the area; and so many who do not work for the prisons work to supply the wants of those who do. The hillside above the town contains the graves of those who have been executed, many thousands of gray tombstones erected over many acres of ground, each stone engraved with the number of a prisoner, seldom with his name, the single letter "X" for executed, and the date of execution. As one approaches the town, one notes a huge signboard high above the local McDonald's franchise, welcoming visitors to "the home of Old Sparky"—that is, the electric chair that was used for decades and which is now enshrined as the central exhibit of the Texas Prison Museum of Huntsville.

As there is an unvarying procedure for carrying out executions, there is an unvarying procedure for those who have come to stand in solidarity with the condemned. The family and friends of the man (or woman) to be executed must wait in a hospice run by the Southern Baptists. They are given no choice in this matter, for the mixture of government and religion in Texas is pervasive—and not just religion as a category, nor even Christianity as a category, but a peculiar version of extreme Calvinism, full of self-justification, retribution, and even cruelty. The hospice is decorated throughout with gory scenes of Jesus's passion and death, painted by those about to be executed, often with accompanying notes from the condemned confessing that they are paying their just dues for their sins. This is the ambience that the family and friends of the condemned must endure while they wait to speak one last time with the condemned by telephone.

While Sheila and the others waited, they were assailed by a particularly antipathetic chaplain, a Catholic, who rattled on about what an awful sin murder is and that murder by abortion is the worst of all. Dominique had refused a chaplain, saying that they were all compromised. If they didn't go along with the system, they wouldn't have been named chaplains here.

Sheila, her cell phone clutched in her hand, was still hoping for a last-minute miracle because that very morning U.S. District Judge Nancy Atlas had issued a stay of execution on the grounds that ballistics evidence used to convict Dominique may have been inaccurate. Some 280 boxes of improperly stored and cataloged evidence, involving some eight thousand cases, covering more than two decades, and kept by the Houston Police Department crime lab, had recently been discovered and could contain information relevant to the case. Harold Hurtt, the Houston police chief, had called for a moratorium on executions in cases like Dominique's, where the lab was involved. A second petition, using the same argument, was before the Supreme Court. The chaplain, claiming that it would be a felony to bring a cell phone into the prison itself, tried to wrestle Sheila's from her. She refused to let go of it, shouting at him that he was interfering with her legal rights and those of Dominique. She won the tussle.

But the call that finally came through advised her that the 5th Circuit Court of Appeals had done what it normally does: it had overturned the stay of execution in response to the objection of Texas's attorney general. There was still the U.S. Supreme Court to be heard from. Meanwhile, the chaplain—"a total ass," as Sheila labeled him—was keeping up his steady babble, apparently believing that the silence everybody desperately wished for would be inappropriate.

The phone conversations with Dominique, when they occurred at last, were so brief as to be all but undetectable. But Sheila was to have some final communications with Dominique after she entered the Walls Unit itself, the section of the prison where executions are carried out, where she was shocked to see that in an interior courtyard a garden had been planted. "He's like a flower opening," she recalled the archbishop's words. Then, once again she was talking to Dominique with a glass barrier between them: "There is Dominique standing up by himself in the cell, and other people, the guards, were close by. We talked very quietly, and I told him that we hadn't heard from the Supreme Court yet and that every moment that went by was good for us. And he said, 'I'm going to be O.K.' He was reassuring me. He was unbelievable. And it was all about making sure to thank everybody. Thank you for being my family, for Patrick coming to see me. I had such a good time with him that day. And thank Andy. And thank Tom. And thank Sant'Egidio: where would I ever have been without them? I would never have met you. And to think Archbishop Tutu came here. Nobody thinks we're anything but he came from South Africa. And on and on. He said, 'You've done so much in such a short time. If I had had you from the beginning, I'd never be here. So know that. If you'd been my lawyer at the trial, they would have listened to you.' Then they came and got me and I had to go back and then I said I gotta talk to him one more time, I have to talk to Dominique one more time, there is something I have to tell him. So they let me."

By this point Sheila was on the verge of hysteria, weeping into the phone to Dominique: "I just want you to know that here I am in my sixties, if anyone's life should be taken it should be mine, because I've had a life. I'm a mother and a grandmother and a wife. All the things you haven't had a chance to do I've had a chance to do." To which Dominique replied, "Sheila, you stop talking like that. You know you're just being silly. You stop that. Where I'm going I'm going to take care of everybody, and you're going to keep up the struggle. You have to stay here and keep up the struggle."

"I'll do the best I can," said Sheila, dripping tears.

Andy got on the phone with Dominique and they joked together as they always had, though by this point Andy was probably more of a wreck inside than Sheila. Then the news came through of the Supreme Court's refusal. Sheila took the phone once more to tell Dominique. Then she said, "I will be with you tonight and I will be with you every minute."

"And I thought," said Sheila recently, as if these things had happened only yesterday, "I've just got to get in there and be as close to him as I can and never take my eyes off him. Never. And that's what I did."

Facing the execution room are two other rooms, one for reporters and for supporters of the condemned man, explicitly invited by him, the other set aside by law for the family of the victim. Both rooms are shielded from the execution room only by panes of glass, so that the viewers may have unobstructed views of the progress of the execution. On this night the second room was empty. No member of the dissenting Lastrapes family had been invited to attend the execution.

The witnesses Dominique had invited were Sheila, Andy, Dave Atwood, and two women who had had lengthy correspondences with him—Barbara Bacci, a Roman woman who collaborated with Sant'Egidio, and Lorna Kelly, a Sant'Egidio member from New York. Each of their names was called out by a prison official, and they were told to proceed to the room from which they would view the execution. Dominique did not invite his mother because he was afraid she would make a scene; he did not invite Jessica because he believed it would be impossible for her to bear. But the first person called as a witness that evening was Archbishop Desmond Tutu. Dominique knew the archbishop could not be there, but forcing the prison officials to call out his name and acknowledge him was a final demonstration by Dominique of his sense of his own dignity and self-worth.

When the witnesses file into the room, they see the condemned already strapped down on a cross-shaped gurney, his arms outstretched, the intravenous tubes by which the chemicals will travel already implanted in his veins. "When we came in," said Sheila, "he looked at me—I think the whole time. I never took my eyes off him and he never took his eyes off me."

An official placed a microphone near Dominique's mouth. Sheila thought his face looked swollen and wondered if he had been already given some sort of medication. His last words, a bit rambling and primitive, suggest that she was right. His initial comment about the number of people present even suggests he may have seen people who weren't there. Certainly, he knew there were thousands praying for him at that moment at an all-night vigil in the Basilica of Santa Maria.

"Yes," he began. "Man, there is a lot of people there. There was a lot of people that got me to this point, and I can't thank them all. But thank you for your love and support. They have allowed me to do a lot more than I could have done on my own. Sheila, I wish I would have met you seven years ago; it would have been a lot easier. But I have overcome a lot. I am not angry but I am disappointed that I was denied justice. But I am happy that I was afforded you all as family and friends. You all have been there for me; it's a miracle. I love you. And I have to tell Jessica I am sorry. I never knew it would come to this. Lorna, you know you have to keep my struggle going. I know you just lost your baby, but you have to keep running. Dave, keep the struggle going. Andy, I love you, man. Tell Andre and them that I didn't get a chance to reach my full potential, but you can help them reach theirs. You needed me, but I just did not know how to be there for them. There is so much

I have to say, but I just can't say it all. I love you all. Please just keep the struggle going. If you turn your back on me, you turn your back on them. I love you all and I'll miss you all. Thanks for allowing me to touch so many hearts. I never knew I could do it, but you made it possible. I am just sorry. And I am not as strong as I thought I was going to be. But I guess it only hurts for a little while. You all are my family. Please keep my memory alive."

Though the Houston Police Department may keep flawed records and the entire justice establishment of Texas may be astonishingly barbaric in its operations, the records kept of Huntsville executions are exceedingly exact:

OFFENDER:	Green Dominique #999068
EXECUTION DATE:	October 26, 2004
TAKEN FROM HOLDING CELL:	7:37 TIME
STRAPPED TO GURNEY:	7:39 TIME
SOLUTION FLOWING:	7:40 RIGHT ARM
	7:41 LEFT ARM
LAST STATEMENT:	7:47 TIME
LETHAL DOSE BEGAN:	7:50 TIME
LETHAL DOSE COMPLETED:	7:54 TIME
PRONOUNCED DEAD:	7:59 TIME

So seven minutes before he began speaking his last words, a tranquilizing drug was already being pumped into him, followed by a paralyzing drug, followed by heart-stopping poison.

Outside the prison at just about 8 P.M., the many protesters gathered there witnessed their own epiphany. The night sky was rent by a dramatic crack of lightning, though the sky was clear and the moon full. Jessica, sure of what the lightning meant, collapsed, falling into the arms of the Lastrapes brothers.

Andre Lastrapes showed his anger to reporters: "I felt it was dirty, and the state will have their chance to face a higher authority—that is, God. The hell with Texas and the justice system. They were full of shit, and I am speaking from my heart. I really mean that. I mean, Andrew Lastrapes was my daddy in the first place, and I forgave Dominique. I know God has a place for Dominique in heaven. The person I met doesn't deserve to die. He became close to me, and I pray that he goes to heaven."

Andy Lofthouse, a witness to the execution, found he could not face the actual moment and turned his back to Dominique. Sheila, exhausted by her tears, was pretty much cried out, but Andy, determined not to give Texas the satisfaction of tears, was lacerated by invisible wounds and had to get himself out of there. He drove off as soon as he could, not realizing he had Jessica's car keys—which left her stranded. She and the Lastrapes brothers rode back to Houston that night with Sheila and her husband, Patrick Racey, who had stood in the parking lot with the other protesters when they beheld with awe the great crack of lightning in the sky.

I had asked Sheila's assistant, Kathryn, who had my detailed itinerary, to phone me at any hour of the day or night with any news. She reached me a little after 2 A.M. continental European time in the German city of Trier to tell me

Dominique was dead. Good-hearted Kathryn, who had come to know Dominique well over the course of many phone conversations and to love him, was immensely sad but strangely peaceful, believing as she did—with impressive firmness—that Dominique had "escaped" to God. "He got away, as the Irish say."

My hotel faced the extensive ruins of the Porta Nigra, an elaborate gate built by the empire-building Romans about A.D. 180 and intended to call attention to the importance of Trier, "Roma Secunda" as the Romans called it, the first city to be founded in Roman-occupied Germany. After I had said good-bye to Kathryn, I looked out across the well-lit night to the huge stone blocks, some weighing as much as six metric tons, assembled more than eighteen centuries before. Most of the stones are still in place, cut and laid there without mortar by slaves.

The Romans were intensely proud of their accomplishments, and they built the longest-lasting empire the world has ever known. They were also insanely cruel, crucifying anyone who got in their way, delighting in the many grisly deaths and the constant flow of human blood that filled their arenas. Though they knew they were great, they didn't know they were cruel. That was something they kept carefully hidden from themselves.

6

"Did he do it?" is the question I inevitably hear from anyone to whom I tell Dominique's story. My answer is that I don't think so, but I am not equipped to provide a definitive answer.

Dominique usually insisted that he was not present when Andrew Lastrapes was shot. Is this possible? Yes. There is nothing in the case's meager evidence to prove that Dominique was present. The only thing that points to him as present (and as the shooter) is the testimony of three fellow robbers, who were as far from being disinterested observers as one could find and who had every reason to collaborate in pointing the finger at Dominique, the youngest and least protected of their quartet. Dominique's father, admittedly not an indifferent witness— though not as patently incredible as the three robbers— signed an affidavit that Dominique was at home with him at the time of the shooting.

But Dominique also told Andy Lofthouse that " 'nobody who ever admitted to doing anything ever got out of here.' And he said that on repeated occasions. He said 'I've been here a long time and I've never seen anybody who ever admitted to anything ever get out of here.' " This leads me to speculate that it is also possible that Dominique was present but was not the shooter, but that he also decided as a legal strategy not to admit this.

Dominique's impatient insistence on locating the tape of that night's events from the convenience store in front of which Andrew Lastrapes was shot certainly points us in the direction of one of the two scenarios above, since Dominique was certain that such a tape would exonerate him by showing another (whom he was unwilling to name) to have been the shooter. One could, I suppose, theorize that this was merely a ploy by Dominique, since he must have known that such a tape would long ago have been rendered useless, either by having been destroyed or by its contents having been taped over.

But Dominique's agitation on the subject of taped evidence goes back far beyond the appearance of Sheila Murphy on the scene. I am in possession of a pitiable letter written by Dominique in August 1994, barely a year after his conviction, complaining—to the first court-appointed attorney assigned to represent him in his appeals—that the tape *must* be found and pointing out that this is his *third* request. Given the faulty memory of his original lawyer, Melamed, and the refusal of Melamed's colleague, Diana Olvera, to be interviewed, there is no way of proving that Dominique asked them to locate such a tape, but the letter of 1994 surely points in that direction.

My own hunch is that one of the above scenarios, more likely the second, comes closest to what happened on that night. But I must admit that it is not outside the realm of possibility that Dominique was the shooter. The difficulty of properly accounting for real lives in cases like these is steeped in far more ambiguities, loose ends, dead ends, and unknowables than one would ever encounter on, say, American television's *Law and Order*. And when the evidence has been manipulated, suppressed, destroyed, forgotten, the obstacles to ascertaining the truth are very nearly insurmountable. It would be easier today to prove that the recently discovered dark matter of the universe is made of baba ghanoush than to prove the innocence of Dominique Green.

But why do we fixate on his innocence? On the "did he do it?" aspect of the case? What I see in the eyes of those who ask this question is that, if I cannot say unequivocally that Dominique was innocent, they are freed from any responsibility toward him. "Oh, well, who knows whether he did it or not, so let's talk about something else."

But the first question an inquiring American should ask is not "Did he do it?" but "Did he receive a fair trial?" And the second question is like it: "Were his subsequent encounters with the law fair?" That is what we would wish, even what we would demand, for ourselves. To both these questions the answer must be a resounding no. His trial was monstrously unfair. And his subsequent encounters with the law were tragic farces, cat-and-mouse games played out in a legal arena run by people who had no intention of giving him justice.

Just prior to Dominique's execution, Andy Lofthouse, a brilliant law student whose deep involvement in this case probably cost him the editorship of the law review at Chicago's John Marshall Law School, was desperately leaving no stone unturned, hoping he might uncover some new route to a stay for Dominique. With nearly quixotic enterprise, he resolved to try once more to speak with Diana Olvera, who had acted as assistant counsel in Dominique's trial but had turned aside all of his and Sheila's requests to be interviewed. ("We tried to contact [her] probably ten times but she would never talk to us.") He visited her office and was horrified to discover that she was now sharing an office with an attorney who had recently been hired to represent Michael Neal, one of those who originally fingered Dominique as Lastrapes's murderer. Michael Neal was already serving a thirty-year sentence. Why, Andy wondered, did he suddenly require a lawyer just as Dominique's case was being reviewed for the last time? Why was one of Dominique's original lawyers, who would never speak about her involvement in Dominique's case, now sharing an office with Neal's lawyer? And why was Olvera, despite the fact that she would not speak to Dominique's current lawyers, willing to sign an affidavit rebutting all of Dominique's charges of ineffective counsel, when it had been so obvious that the principal lawyer, Melamed, had been ineffective? Was there any way that all of this could be just coincidence?

The pitiable letter I mentioned above is dreary additional

evidence that, very early in the game, the door to justice had been firmly shut on Dominique. The letter is worth quoting in full to demonstrate the powerless vacuum in which Dominique found himself. Recall in reading it that at the time of writing Dominique was just twenty, a very young man whose only experiences were ghetto experiences, most of them negative. He was just beginning to develop an awareness of his true existential situation—of the inescapable trap in which he was now confined. Whereas he seems during his trial to have believed mistakenly that he was playing a kind of game that would soon end either in his release or in a relatively brief prison term, in this letter he has begun to account his conviction as a deadly serious matter and is attempting to summon the critical intelligence necessary to defeat the system in which he is trapped. But he is, as yet, rather far from the eloquence he would later develop. I reprint the letter here with its typos, misspellings, and other verbal peculiarities:

Michael P. Fosher
August 31st, 1994
The Lyric Center
440 Louisiana #2100
Houston, Texas 77002

Re: Information, Records, Documents of the trial of,
Dominique Green, that he wishes to obtain and review that
is presently in your possession which is the main primary
objective of his concern.

Dear Michael Fosher:

Months and months have past since I last chose to write you asking for information regarding my case. And also sending material to you that I had hoped to help you. But somehow you failed to reply to my requests or even give me a responce. So with the utmost amount of patience, I have chosen to write to you again seeking the materials that I have requested, and am now requesting from you.

As you know, Mr. Fosher, I have sent you my two indictments. One is for aggravated robbery, and the other is for the crime I am charged with committing and convicted for, capital murder. When I had sent them to you some time ago, I also sent you alot of information I gathered from researching cases which I sincerely felt would affect or have an affect on the surface of my two indictments.

Also in my earlier stages of writing I also pointed out to you the importance to me it was of obtaining for my research my trial transcript and statement of facts, and also my co-defendants confessions. The trial record as a whole, but you also failed to comply and/or respond.

I have stressed the importance of all of this by even becoming some what hysterical or aggravated with you in one of my past letters of communication. Although, I did not mean to become blatantly upset. It just appeared to me that you did not feel as strongly about the value of my life that I did and still do. But, I do apologize for the hysteria.

But in regard to the other matters that I am writing

about. I would only hope that you can fulfill my needs for this information.

In due time I have considered to began researching and fighting my case for my own personal interest. I am aware that there are certain issues that I cannot raise on direct appeal simply because they were never raised at my trial. So I would like to have all the information and documents either filed on my behalf or present to the trial court that convicted and sentenced me to death. By my trial attorneys, Sanford Melameade and Diana Olivera, so I can be knowledgeable of what issues are raisable and the others that are not raisable. Instead of taking someones word for it.

I also seek and hope for you to return my indictments to me along with any cases information that I may have sent to you. So that I may begin my research again. I have not been able to because everything that I have sent to you, you have kept them. But however you fail to reply to my letters.

I also would appreciate it if you could take time out to send my trial records at your convienance which I hope is as soon as possible. If not the original could you at least send me a duplicate copy of everything in your possession regarding my case. I fully understand that this information must be in your possession, because you are currently in association with handling my case on direct appeal. For possible appellant relief through the Court of Criminal Appeals or via Writ of Habeas Corpus.

My last concern regards a videotape from a store my co-defendants mentioned during my trial to implicate me as being with them that time the murder I am charged with committing was committed. I also brought this to your attention in at least two letters I had written to you when I had first begin writing to you sometime ago.

However you mentioned nothing about that either. Instead I met a attorney that was and is helping me with my case to the best of all of his abilities. But a problem lies with obtaining this videotape. I feel that since you were appointed to my case and he works for a law firm, you would have less difficulties retracting this videotape. I was informed by him that his firm wont allow any use of funds for my investigation until my case has been ruled on. But obviously since you are appointed by the state. The state would have to afford you the cost of a investigator to go and recieve this critical evidence. I say critical, because the tape wont not only prove I was not involved, it would clearly exonerate me of this crime. So could you please contact Brent E. Newton, (713) 522-5917, For more details about this videotape. Because as I understand it each store has a different policy about their videotapes. I am concerned that by the I am eligible for funds to be meted out for investigators to help me that corporate policy may expire for the keeping of such store videotapes. Then I will be left with no actual proof of innocense only doubt.

I again humbly and respectfully implore you to fulfill my needs with the information, documents, etc.. that I have requested. Or will also later request to further assist me. Before matters become extremely, to late.

I sincerely appreciate the time you have afforded me in reading this communication. I also know and respect the fact that you have numerous other cases that demand your time and attention. But please give this letter the respect and consideration I feel it deserves.

I look forward to hearing from you soon.

Sincerely,

Dominique Green #999068
ELLIS I UNIT G-15
HUNTSVILLE, TX 77343

cc: file

This letter gives us a hint of the immensity of the forces that a poor convict is up against and of the anguish of the losing situation that an intelligent but resourceless person is likely to find himself in should he have the misfortune to be convicted—or even accused—of a crime in the State of Texas. Dominique is begging—and has been begging for a full year—to receive documents that would have been given him as a matter of course elsewhere. Similarly, his urgent requests that the acquitting security tape from the convenience store be located and viewed have fallen on deaf ears. What is going on here? Why is the lawyer so unresponsive?

In the issue released just before Dominique's execution, *Texas Monthly* featured a courageous article by Michael Hall entitled "And Justice for Some," which lifted the veil on the Texas justice system. Sheila, who always felt she was leaving the United States when she journeyed into Texas, read the article and thought that at last she understood what had been transpiring all along. I remind the reader that one Texas court, the Court of Criminal Appeals (CCA), the highest criminal court in the state, which handles all criminal appeals (while the Texas Supreme Court handles civil matters), was responsible for denying several of Dominique's most important appeals (see page 32).

As revealed in the *Texas Monthly* article, this court is "ruled by a bunch of pro-prosecutor, right-wing ideologues with one goal in mind: keeping inmates behind bars no matter what." Tom Price, a (usually dissenting) judge on the court, calls it "a national laughingstock." But it is no laughing matter to the many petitioners whose cases Michael Hall recounts: for instance, Roy Criner, a twenty-one-year-old logger, whom the CCA meant to keep in prison forever, even though multiple DNA tests proved that he did not commit the rape he was convicted of; Ernest Willis, drugged with powerful antipsychotic medicines in the months before his trial, "turning him into a drooling zombie, something the prosecutor made full use of in front of the jury"; and many, many other defendants.

The unfortunate Willis was convicted of setting fire to a house in a Texas town that killed two women. When his appeals attorneys uncovered evidence of the drugging, as well as evidence withheld by the prosecutor, both of which Willis's court-appointed attorney had gone along with, his trial judge wrote a thirty-three-page opinion recommending a new trial, which the CCA turned down. A federal judge intervened in

2000 to remove Willis from Death Row—the first inmate to walk free in nearly four years. Without question, the judges of the CCA knew that Willis was innocent, but their policy was not to let anyone go. Roy Criner escaped their clutches only because the PBS show *Frontline* featured his case in an episode called "The Case for Innocence." This was also in 2000, and the notoriety occasioned by the program that summer clashed with George W. Bush's aspiration to be president. So the then governor made a single exception to his oft-stated policy of abiding by the decisions of the CCA and released Criner.

In 1994, "on the heels of Bush's successful run for governor," writes Hall, "Republicans swept into statewide office." Among those swept in was a little-known lawyer named Sharon Keller, now well-known as "Sharon Killer," who was soon to become the CCA's "philosophical leader" and in 2000 its presiding judge. Her mission, in part, has been to refuse reviews and re-trials to anyone who could not "establish innocence"—a totally new standard and one that is virtually impossible to meet. More and more, writes Hall, the judges of the CCA were "ex-prosecutors whose main goal seemed to be to satisfy the state's appetite for execution." It may come as a surprise to non-Texans that "the judges on the CCA are elected politicians," who get themselves elected by being "careful to paint themselves as tough on crime and criminals, whatever the cost."

Judge Keller's rulings have been consistently shocking. When, for instance, the case of Cesar Fierro, a Mexican immigrant, came before her, it was because it had been discovered, after Fierro had spent fifteen years in prison, that he had confessed to murdering an El Paso taxi driver only because the local police had told him that if he didn't confess, their Mexican colleagues across the border in Juarez would torture his mother and stepfather, whom they had taken into custody. Keller's conclusion: "We conclude that applicant's due process rights were violated. But, because we conclude that the error was harmless, we deny relief." By this move, Keller actually changed the standard in capital habeas cases, making the effective use of habeas corpus virtually impossible.

Fierro has now been on Death Row for twenty-eight years and, as I write these words, is facing imminent execution, despite the recent affliction of serious mental illness. There is simply no evidence that he committed the murder. "This," said a heroic Texas lawyer who has spent much of his life defending indigents, "is a brutally tragic case." Perhaps Keller's most famous denial of a stay of execution was in the case of Karla Faye Tucker, who made the mistake of asking George W. Bush for mercy, a plea that he ridiculed notoriously to the journalist Tucker Carlson after her execution.

Hall makes the obvious recommendation that the CCA should be disbanded and its duties to rule on requests for review turned over to the state's Supreme Court, as is done in every other state except Oklahoma. A central problem of the Texas system, however, aside from the current predisposition of the CCA judges, is that the state has no set standards for the appellate lawyers whom the CCA appoints to handle criminal appeals. Till recently—and of course at the time of Dominique's trial—it had no set standards even for court-appointed trial lawyers nor any set procedures for appointing them! Orlando Garcia, a federal district judge, has spoken out against the arbitrariness of the way the CCA appoints lawyers to represent poor clients: "My biggest concern with the court is how it goes about appointing lawyers. Who does that? Is there an application? Or does any judge just add any attorney he wants?" In one of the cases that came before him, Garcia granted a stay of execution after deciding that the CCA's appointment of the lawyer was "a cynical and reprehensible attempt to expedite petitioner's execution at the expense of all semblance of fairness and integrity."

"A good lawyer," writes Hall, "can save a man's life, or at least give him a fair shot. A bad lawyer or just an inexperienced one—intimidated by the state's staff of efficient assistant DAs, ignorant of the art of investigation or the fine points of evidence, overwhelmed by the paperwork and deadlines—can send a man to Death Row." Texas's penchant for paying its lawyers a pittance to defend indigent clients (in contrast to the substantial funds expended by comparable states, such as California) hardly helps matters. The truth is that Dominique never had a fair shot; he never even had a chance. He was convicted and executed by a system that has no regard for fairness and no regard for human life.

Well, that may be too broad a charge. This system seems to have had quite a lot of regard for the life of Patrick Haddix, the white coconspirator. But it is a system that regularly—and we might even say, as a matter of course—discriminates against the poor and minorities (and God help you if you're poor *and* a member of a minority). As a young, conscientious, white lawyer told me with almost uncontrollable rage in his voice, "In Texas, the object is to fry as many niggers as possible."

Since 1976, when a more conservative U.S. Supreme Court once again gave the go-ahead to state executions (after some years in which the practice had been deemed "cruel and unusual" under a more liberal Court consensus), Texas has succeeded in executing 425 people, all poor, most from minorities. The next largest state count is Virginia's, with 102 executions. After that, the numbers (at least outside the South) drop sharply, while many states (and more each year) have stopped executing altogether.

Even in Texas, there is not a uniform thirst for execution. By far the most executions stem from sentences in Harris County, where Houston is located and where Dominique was tried.* Recently, Harris County District Attorney Chuck Rosenthal, an ethnic Jew whose membership as a Southern Baptist had greatly helped his rise to political prominence, had

---

* Till lately, Dallas County vied with Harris for the distinction of being the most unjust county in Texas. But Dallas now has as its district attorney Craig Watkins, the first black district attorney in Texas history. Watkins has partnered with the Innocence Project (see Chapter 7) in reviewing DNA evidence from old convictions—convictions won in cases tried by the legendary Henry Wade (of *Roe v. Wade*), who served as Dallas County's district attorney for thirty-seven years and regularly withheld exculpatory evidence from the defense and from the jury. During Wade's tenure it was well-known that if you were charged with a crime, you were almost certain to be convicted. So far, the convictions of seventeen prisoners have been overturned on the basis of DNA reviews; one prisoner, James Woodard, had served more than twenty-seven years in prison before his exoneration. Two hundred fifty additional cases remain under review.

to step down after a series of his racist e-mail messages was made public. (Also, sexist e-mails. What a surprise.)

The conduct of criminal law in Texas is a judgment not only on Texas but on all American lawyers and jurists and, in the end, on all Americans. Texas, after all, is not a foreign country but an integral part of the United States of America. It is not enough to bemoan the strange vindictiveness of Texans, then wring one's hands and turn to other things. (Are we satisfied that justice should thus depend on geography?) Nor is it enough to limit one's attention only to the use of the death penalty, whether in Texas or elsewhere. The terrible fate of Dominique was bound up in a skein of ugly, mismatched threads, which are the social causes of his suffering and death.

The first, and perhaps the most obvious, cause may be found in society's indifference to its threatened children. How easily we ignore the cry of poor, abused, and neglected children. How few are the effective programs of intervention that we have created to help them and their confused, beset, screwed-up parents. The Mexican-American journalist Joe Loya—a friend of mine, a softhearted soul who spent many years in prison for his role as the fearsome Beirut Bandit, who had a long winning streak robbing banks up and down California—once said to me, "I never met a man in prison who had not been beaten by his father or his mother or abused or abandoned." Are we really so dull-witted, so uncreative a society that we can come up with no better response to the plight of such children than the inadequate social welfare programs sponsored by most states, as our governments bide their time till these unfortunate children grow old enough to be incarcerated?

A second cause may be found in our indifference to criminal law and to legal procedures that we assume will never involve us (so why should we need to be concerned?). The way our society treats its most vulnerable and unprotected citizens is a judgment on all of us who have the money to purchase and read a book—and therefore are likely to have the money to purchase adequate legal assistance. We all need to familiarize ourselves with the injustices that have been done—and continue to be done—in our name.

In addition to the necessary reform of criminal law and of legal protections for indigent and near indigent defendants, we have an obligation to protect prisoners from arbitrary indignities and cruelty. There is no good reason, for instance, that Death Row inmates must be kept in solitary confinement. Desmond Tutu nailed it when he called that a form of torture.

So in the last section of this book, I make a few suggestions for your continued reflection and involvement in three areas of our social life: the protection of children, the end of the death penalty, and the humane reform of prisons. The first list offers additional books, reports, and Web sites that some readers may wish to consult. The second list offers a short series of organizations, one or more of which you may wish to join and support with contributions of money and/or labor, or from which you may wish to request assistance for a project in your community.

It may be stated unequivocally that there are no good arguments in favor of the death penalty. On the one hand, it is not a true deterrent, since states without the death penalty inevitably have far lower murder rates than do states that allow capital punishment. Life without parole, on the other hand, always holds out the possibility that subsequent evidence will exonerate a condemned prisoner. If he has already been executed, an eventual reversal of his conviction will be more ironic than exonerating. The likely estimate is that one in every eight prisoners executed is innocent. Life without parole costs a state much less than does an execution. A 2005 New Jersey report, for instance, found that the state's death penalty has cost taxpayers $253 million since 1983 without succeeding in executing anyone. This is because New Jersey's safeguards for criminals are more generous than those of Texas—that is, more fair—but all states that execute spend considerably more on executions than they would have spent on life without parole.

The figures cited here may easily be confirmed by consulting the Death Penalty Information Center and other reputable sources. The reason that it costs far more to execute a prisoner than to keep him in prison for life lies in the state's costs in responding to the legal appeals that the prisoner files subsequent to his conviction. The Joint Legislative Budget Committee of the California Legislature, for instance, found in 1999 that "elimination of the death penalty would result in a net savings to the state of at least several tens of millions of dollars annually, and a net savings to local governments in the millions to tens of millions of dollars on a statewide basis." While it would be possible to shorten the appeals process, this could be accomplished only by eliminating the protections guaranteed to every citizen by the U.S. Constitution.

That states that execute tend to execute the poor and minorities is an assertion not open to contradiction. As Supreme Court Justice Harry Blackmun said in 1994, "Even under the most sophisticated death penalty statutes, race continues to play a major role in determining who shall live and who shall die." About 40 percent of the people on Texas Death Row are black, as opposed to 12 percent of the general Texas population. As for the race sensitivity of our criminal justice system, it has been shown that even prosecutors in Philadelphia, where one might expect race to play a lesser role, attempt to remove 52 percent of potential black jurors while trying to remove only 23 percent of all other potential jurors. If they do this in the green tree of Pennsylvania, the racially stacked juries of dry-tree Texas should come as no surprise.

Almost all Christian churches are now opposed to the death penalty on moral grounds—the most prominent exception being the Southern Baptists, who constitute the second largest Christian denomination in the United States.* Once

---

* The American Baptists, however, are opposed to the death penalty. Disagreements of interpretation over the authentic Baptist tradition, which was once a more oppositional form of Christianity than it tends to be today, have caused many prominent Southern Baptists—including Jimmy Carter, Bill Moyers, and Bill Clinton—to leave the fold or to rethink their commitment. The novelist John Grisham, whose fictions have done so much to dramatize the moral dilemmas of American life, calls himself "a moderate Baptist" and has said, "I'm a Christian, and

again, as when we found ourselves in the hospice at Huntsville, we find ourselves faced with a theology of extreme Calvinism that, one cannot help but notice, shares something in common with the cruel urges of primitive peoples toward acts of human sacrifice. A Calvinism that depicts God as demanding the death of his son as expiation for human sin, as arbitrarily assigning some to eternal happiness, others to eternal damnation, may have little trouble offering up some lives—especially those of the poor and marginal—to the executioner. Take him, not me! is the ancient cry of those who believe in a God of vengeance rather than of love.

Which brings us to the title of this book. In what way do I propose Dominique as a saint? Certainly, in the common sense of the word, "saint" as a person of extraordinary kindness and patience. Dominique was hardly a saint in his early years, but I think we may speak of him this way in his last years as a fully achieved human being.

The three largest Christian denominations in the world—Catholics, with more than 1.1 billion adherents; Orthodox, with nearly a quarter billion; and Anglicans, with more than 80 million—together representing two-thirds of the Christians on the planet, all speak of saints as those among the dead who we know are with God and to whom it is therefore ap-

---

you'll never convince me that Jesus taught revenge killings are what Christians are supposed to be doing." On the other hand, many Roman Catholics, despite the stance of their church, favor the death penalty. So there is often enough a significant disjunction between a church's stated position and the opinions of its members.

propriate to speak and to ask that they pray with us whose earthly journeys are unfinished. I would also propose Dominique as a saint in this more theological sense. There are not a few whose lives he touched who view him in this way, who believe they speak to him and that he hears and answers them, even that, as he promised on his last day of life on this earth, "Where I'm going I'm going to take care of everybody."

However that may be, Dominique was not buried in Huntsville's brutal burial ground. His ashes were brought to Rome by Dave Atwood and his wife, Priscilla, and today they rest in the shadow of the beautiful Basilica of Santa Maria in Trastevere, in the dignified entrance hall to a seventeenth-century palace, which is now the home of Sant'Egidio's refuge for abused and abandoned children. His carved memorial stone reads:

DOMINIQUE J. GREEN
HOUSTON 13 V 1974–HUNTSVILLE 26 X 2004
BROTHER AND FRIEND

It is the Lord who sets out the steps of a man
and takes pleasure in his journey.
Though he fall, he will not be sent sprawling—
For the Lord is holding him by the hand.
Psalm 37

7

WOULD YOU LIKE TO KNOW MORE?

Here are a few books, articles, and Web sites you may wish to consult.

No Equal Justice: Race and Class in the American Criminal Justice System, by David Cole (New Press, 2000). An examination of all aspects of our judicial system, including police behavior, jury selection, and sentencing; a convincing case that there is a double standard that allows those with money to enjoy constitutional protections not extended to those without money. A 2003 article with some updates can be found at http://www.nacdl.org/public.nsf/GideonAnniversary/news04?opendocument/

Slavery by Another Name: The Re-Enslavement of Black Americans from the Civil War to World War II, by Douglas A. Blackmon (Doubleday, 2008). An exposé of the little-known but widespread American practice of convict leasing. "Under laws enacted specifically to intimidate blacks, tens of thousands of African Americans were arbitrarily arrested, hit with outrageous fines, and charged for the costs of their own arrests. With no means to pay these ostensible 'debts,' prisoners were sold as forced laborers to coal mines, lumber camps, brickyards, railroads, quarries and farm plantations." The author's Web site is at http://slaverybyanothername.com/

The Trouble with Black Boys . . . And Other Reflections on Race, Equity, and the Future of Public Education, by Pedro A. Noguera (Jossey-Bass, 2008). In this series of essays, Noguera illustrates the societal assumptions and pressures black boys face as they grow up and shows how these assumptions often lead to poor choices by the boys, choices that ultimately fulfill the low expectations society and the educational system set for them. A scholarly but very readable book that offers recommendations on how our educational system could better deal with this syndrome.

Debating the Death Penalty: Should America Have Capital Punishment?, edited by Hugo Adam Bedau and Paul G. Cassell (Oxford University Press, 2004). A collection of essays by federal judges, lawyers, and philosophers consisting of four essays supporting the death penalty and four arguing against. The essays take into account race and economics, retribution and morality, the risks of wrongful convictions, the deterrence value of capital punishment, and closure for victims' families.

"A Deadly Distinction: Harris County Is a Pipeline to Death Row," by Mike Tolson (*Houston Chronicle*, February 5, 2001). This article can be

found at http://www.chron.com/disp/story.mpl/special/penalty/813783
.html

The Innocent Man: Murder and Injustice in a Small Town, by John Grisham
(Dell, 2007). A true story of routine injustice in our criminal justice system
(this time in Oklahoma), by the famous author of legal thrillers.

Dallas Morning News. Its investigative series on sexual abuse in Texas's juvenile institutions can be viewed at: http://www.dallasnews.com/investigative
reports/tyc/

Thomas Cahill's Web site. Additional information about Dominique Green,
his case, and his world may be found at http://www.thomascahill.com/

Bill Moyers Journal. Part of an interview with Dominique Green can be
found at http://www.pbs.org/moyers/journal/blog/2007/12/dominique
_green_in_his_own_wor.html

DPIC: Death Penalty Information Center. http://www.deathpenalty
info.org/

WOULD YOU LIKE TO DO MORE?

Here are some organizations you may wish to join and/or
support, or from which you may wish to seek assistance for
your own community.

Childhelp
http://www.childhelp.org/

Founded in 1959, Childhelp works to meet the needs of abused, neglected, and at-risk children. Services include residential centers and/or counseling programs in seven states, as well as national programs such as Good-Touch/ Bad-Touch, Children's Advocacy Centers, and the National Child Abuse Hotline, 1-800-4-A-CHILD (1-800-422-4453), which provides free crisis intervention and child abuse counseling from professional counselors twenty-four hours a day. The hotline counselors also provide referrals to local agencies and adult survivor groups throughout the United States and Canada.

Pro-Vision Ministries, Inc.

http://www.provision-inc.org/index.htm

Founded in 1989 by Roynell Young, a former defensive back for the Philadelphia Eagles, Pro-Vision is based in Houston with the mission, according to Young, to "interrupt the pipeline that is causing young men to go from the cradle to prison." The organization runs three programs: Manhood Development, which provides life management and other skills; the Pro-Vision School, an all-male charter middle school with teachers trained in motivating at-risk kids to learn; and the Enterprise Academy, which teaches members financial and job skills with on-the-job training. Within each of these programs the families of members can also receive benefits, such as mental health counseling and job training.

Perspectives

http://www.perspectives-family.org/

An award-winning, multiprogram human service agency based in St. Louis Park, Minnesota, and providing comprehensive services to hundreds of homeless and at-risk families in the Minneapolis area. Its purpose is total family recovery through the breaking of cycles of social and psychological destructiveness. At present, its programs are unique in their comprehensiveness, but Perspectives could serve as a national model.

The Annie E. Casey Foundation

http://www.aecf.org/

Founded in 1948 to meet the needs of vulnerable children and families and in the belief that all children need and deserve a family for life, the Annie E. Casey Foundation makes grants to states, cities, and neighborhoods so they may better meet these needs. The foundation works with youth who end up in the juvenile justice system from impoverished single-parent homes and have high rates of learning disabilities, mental health, or substance abuse problems.

Court Appointed Special Advocates (CASA)

National: http://www.nationalcasa.org/

Texas: http://www.texascasa.org/

Trains community volunteers to speak for the best interests of abused and neglected children in court.

Southern Center for Human Rights

http://www.schr.org/

Founded in 1976, the Southern Center for Human Rights's legal work includes representing prisoners in challenges to unconstitutional conditions and practices in prisons and jails, challenging systemic failures in the legal representation of poor people in the criminal courts, and representing people facing the death penalty who otherwise would have no representation. The center also opposes the privatization of prisons and correctional functions.

The Innocence Project

http://www.innocenceproject.org/

Founded in 1992, the Innocence Project assists prisoners who could be proven innocent through DNA testing. As of July 2008, it has assisted in the exoneration of 218 people in the United States, each of whom served an average of twelve years in prison, including 16 who served time on Death Row.

NCADP: National Coalition to Abolish the Death Penalty

http://www.ncadp.org/

Founded in 1976 in response to the Supreme Court decision in *Gregg v. Georgia*, which permitted executions to resume in the United States, it supports efforts to abolish the death penalty in this country and throughout the world.

Texas Coalition to Abolish the Death Penalty

http://www.tcadp.org/

An inclusive organization, founded by Dave Atwood, composed of human rights activists, crime victims and their families, Death Row prisoners and their families, persons working within the criminal justice system, persons opposed to capital punishment on religious and moral grounds, and other concerned citizens opposed to capital punishment.

A portion of the author's proceeds from the sale of this book will be donated to the Texas Coalition to Abolish the Death Penalty.

A SUMMARY OF THE CASE OF
DOMINIQUE GREEN

This summary of Dominique's case, written by Andrew Lofthouse in early 2004 at Sheila Murphy's request, was intended to serve as an information sheet to be distributed to the press and other interested parties. I include it here because it is an admirably terse summary of Dominique's story.

HOW RACISM AND A FLAWED LEGAL SYSTEM
CONSPIRE TO EXECUTE DOMINIQUE GREEN

Dominique Green is a 29-year-old African American who is nearing the end of his appeals on Texas Death Row. We believe that after a review of the facts of the case, you, like us, will see racism and a flawed legal system prevented justice from prevailing in Dominique's case.

Dominique Green was an unloved, African American young

man, who was poor in spirit as well as material goods. His parents were alcoholics and his father was addicted to marijuana. His mother was mentally ill and repeatedly tortured and physically abused Dominique and his younger brothers, going so far as holding their hands over a flaming stove.

To save his fragile siblings, Dominique took their punishment. Once he took his brother to a homeless shelter where they lived to avoid the constant abuse at home. When Dominique, at age 15, and his younger brother Marlon were thrown out of their house by their mother, Dominique rented a storage shed for the two of them to live in and sold drugs to support Marlon and himself.

One evening in 1992, when Dominique was 18 years old, he allegedly went out with a group of three men whom he knew. They were said to have robbed people at gunpoint. One man, Andrew Lastrapes, was killed by a single shot to the chest.

There were no eyewitnesses or scientific evidence that indicated Dominique participated in this crime. The only evidence against him came from the other young men who all testified against Dominique. In return, the State dropped capital murder charges against them a few days before Dominique's trial. Dominique was also offered a deal in exchange for testimony about the other men, but Dominique refused, saying he was innocent.

Two of the other men, the black men, went to prison, while the white man who admitted being present at the murder and sharing the proceeds from the robberies was not indicted or prosecuted at all. Indeed, prosecutors encouraged him not to speak to anyone about the case, even though he was never charged. This all occurred in Houston, a part of Harris County, Texas, a place that has sent more inmates to their executions than 47 states and has thus gained the infamous title "Death Penalty Capital of the World."

During the sentencing phase of the trial—when the jury was determining whether Dominique should live or die— his court-appointed lawyer chose psychologist Dr. Walter Quijano to testify in defense. To analyze Dominique's future dangerousness, Dr. Quijano took into account the fact that Dominique is African American. He did not, however, share this bias with the jury.

Recently, the Supreme Court overturned the death sentence of Victor Saldano after a former Texas attorney general, John Cornyn, admitted error in multiple cases in which prosecutors called Dr. Quijano, who had testified in a similar capacity as he had in Dominique's trial, saying Mr. Saldano was more likely to be violent because he was Hispanic.

Racism again infected this phase of Dominique's trial when the prosecution construed the words of a rap song to be his own. While Dominique was locked up awaiting trial, he wrote a letter to a friend. At the end of the letter he quoted a popular rap song with the words "trigga happy nigga." Dominique, who was only 18 at the time, meant this as a tongue-in-cheek reference to how he thought the police saw him, not to any future plans.

The jury, which had no African Americans on it, was not

informed the phrase was from a song. The prosecution argued Dominique should be executed because he is a "trigger-happy nigger" even though he had no prior convictions for violent crime and only one shot was fired after an apparent struggle where the victim pulled out a knife.

The "defense" also put Dominique's mother on the stand even though her doctor told them she suffers from psychological problems, including multiple personality disorder, and was not stable. The defense lawyer [in this case, Diana Olvera is meant], however, told the judge that she knew how to determine which personality was testifying. The mother then stated that Dominique should be executed.

The judge in Dominique's case, Judge Shaver, appointed the defense counsels to represent Dominique even though neither one had ever principally represented a defendant charged with the death penalty. In fact, the only other capital case the defense counsel had worked on was the infamous "sleeping lawyer" case that also was before Judge Shaver, who afterwards remarked to the *Los Angeles Times*: "The Constitution entitles you to a lawyer. It doesn't say that the lawyer has to be awake."*

While this may seem like a comedy of errors, unfortunately in Harris County this comedy is performed routinely. No matter what view you may have of the death penalty, all must agree that those facing the ultimate punishment

---

* Shaver's pronouncement has been reported in slightly different words by others (see p. 27) but the import is always the same.

should receive a fair trial, free of racism and incompetent counsel.

Since being convicted, Dominique has grown and matured dramatically, making one wonder just what the state will achieve by executing him. He has helped numerous other inmates to survive the torturous nature of Death Row and has submitted his engaging artwork and poetry in various exhibits around the country and world.

We hope you will find the space in your life to support Dominique as he fights for his life.

ACKNOWLEDGMENTS

I am grateful to many, many people who were helpful to me in the writing of this book, most especially to Sheila Murphy and Andrew Lofthouse, without whom I could not have written much of anything, but also to Jessica Tanksley and David Atwood, both of whose cooperation was invaluable in creating an accurate account. Besides Jessica and David, a number of Houstonians supplied me with important material and insights, among these Dominique's mother, Stephanie, his brothers, Hollingsworth and Marlon—now a sergeant in the U.S. Army, whom I interviewed in Anchorage prior to his second tour of duty in Iraq—and Sylvia Gonzales. Mary C. Schneider, a sympathetic psychologist who interviewed Dominique extensively, was generous with her time and insights, as was Pat Lofthouse with copies of the videotaped interviews she had made of Dominique and of relevant figures in his case.

Gerald Kelly offered me his gracious hospitality at Maryknoll House; and my wife Susan Cahill, Bennett Ashley, Lynn Franklin, Walter Long, Mario Marazziti, James Morris, Michael Smith, Donald Spoto, and Brigid Wolff all read early drafts of the manuscript and offered exceedingly useful criticism. I could not have managed without the marvelous assistance of Sarah C. Palmer, whose research abilities quite surpass my own. As with all my books, there stands behind this one a large cast of essential dramatis personae: Nan A. Talese (always in first place) and her staff, Doubleday's publisher Stephen Rubin, Kathy Trager, Emily Mahon, Jessie Bright, John Pitts, Nora Reichard, Trent Duffy, the incomparable Jennifer Marshall, and the members of the sales force, without whose enthusiasm no author can hope to reach his intended readers. Nor can I omit mention of my preternaturally astute literary agent Lynn Nesbit and her able colleagues.

I would also like to thank Ivan Cantu, Kenneth Foster Jr., Howard Guidry, and Son Tran for permission to reprint excerpts from their writings. Dominique J. Green, before his death, turned over to me copies of all his writings with a view to my using them as I wished to tell his story.

A NOTE ABOUT THE AUTHOR

THOMAS CAHILL is the author of five volumes in the Hinges of History series: *How the Irish Saved Civilization, The Gifts of the Jews, Desire of the Everlasting Hills, Sailing the Wine-Dark Sea,* and *Mysteries of the Middle Ages.* They have been best-sellers, not only in the United States but also in countries ranging from Italy to Brazil. He and his wife, Susan, also a writer, divide their time between New York City and Rome.

A NOTE ABOUT THE TYPE

The text of this book is set in Adobe Jenson. Designed by Robert Slimbach for the family of Adobe Originals historical revivals, its Roman styles are based on a Venetian old-style text face cut by Nicolas Jenson in 1470, while its italic styles are based on the formal cursive forms invented by Ludovico degli Arrighi while he was employed as a scribe at the Papal Chancery in Rome, circa 1415–1422. The resulting font is a highly readable and elegant typeface.